I0762719

TO

FROM

DATE

100 DAYS TO BE *still* AND KNOW

A DEVOTIONAL JOURNAL

100 Days to Be Still and Know: A Devotional Journal

First Edition, January 2026

Published by:

21154 Highway 16 East
Siloam Springs, AR 72761
dayspring.com

Written by: Cleere Cherry Reaves
Cover Design by: Lauren Purtle

Printed in Vietnam
Prime: U4579
ISBN: 979-8-88603-414-1

INTRODUCTION

Welcome to this sacred space—where striving is silenced and stillness makes room for the presence of God.

At first glance, stillness and hope may seem like opposites—one quiet and reflective, the other expectant and forward-reaching. But in the Kingdom of God, they are intimately connected. Hope doesn't grow from hustle. It's not found in the noise or the next thing. It takes root in the pause—in the moments we sit, breathe, and listen for His voice.

This devotional journal is not about performance or checking a box. It's a gentle invitation to come back to the feet of Jesus. To pause long enough to ask, *What is God saying to me right now? What truth does He speak over my identity? How is He shaping me in this season? What is His tone—His posture—toward my pain, my questions, my joy?*

My prayer for these 100 days is that you'll rediscover the art of *abiding*. That these pages will become holy ground—where fear is quieted, faith is nurtured, and the Spirit of God meets you in deeply personal ways.

When life feels heavy or hurried, return here. Let these reflections guide you back to the shadow of His wings—where rest isn't a reward, but a right for the beloved. Here, you are free to marinate in truth, to wrestle, to wonder, to worship.

There is no time wasted at the feet of Jesus. So slow down. Breathe deep. Let yourself be seen. Be held. Be changed. Be still, child. You are in the *safest hands.*

With love and hope,

Claire Cheng Pears

IN THE HANDS OF HOPE

This is how we know that we belong to the truth and how we set our hearts at rest in His presence.
I JOHN 3:19 NIV

We try hard to make things happen on our own, don't we? In our timing. According to our preferences. Aligned with the blueprint we've mapped out in our minds.

In the process, we quietly assume a role that was never ours to take on. We forget His power. We live as though we must alert Him when the waves rise too high or explain our dreams to Him when the waters grow still.

But God—so patient and kind—doesn't shame us for our grasping. He meets us with grace, like a father letting his child sit on his lap and "drive" the car. Wide-eyed and determined, we grip the wheel with tiny hands, unaware that the Father's hands have never left it.

This is our God. Mighty, steady, and always in control. You don't have to co-pilot the plan. You don't need to inform the Infinite or jolt Him awake to your storm. He is already present. Already holding you.

So today, take a breath. Surrender the illusion of control. And remember—His hands have never failed.

day 1

What do you wish you had control of?
What would it look like to hand it over to God today?

Dear Jesus, thank You for being patient in my stubbornness and forgetfulness. You know me intimately, and You lead me perfectly. I place today in Your hands. In Jesus's name, amen.

REMOVING THE BUSY BADGE

The God of peace will soon crush Satan under your feet.
The grace of our Lord Jesus be with you.
ROMANS 16:20 NIV

It's hard to grasp the rhythm of time, isn't it? It slips by more quickly with each passing year. The days felt longer "back then"—slower somehow. There was a steadiness to them. We were more present, more grounded in the moment, more sensitive to what truly mattered.

But somewhere along the way, we began to believe a subtle lie: that busyness equals value, and that a packed calendar equals importance. We stack our commitments like dominoes, hoping they'll lead to significance—yet often all they create is exhaustion. The truth is, hustle doesn't make us holy or meaningful. It just makes us distracted. At the end of our lives, we won't wish we had sent more emails or squeezed in more appointments. We'll long to have loved deeper, lingered longer, and lived with more intention.

So, what if we began planning our days with the Father instead of ahead of Him? What if we stopped wearing "busy" like a badge and started calling our lives full—full of meaning, people, and purpose? When we're tempted to measure our worth by our productivity, may we pause to ask the One who made us to remind us of who we really are!

day 2

What would it look like to become more intentional about the things that matter most?

Dear Jesus, thank You for the value You have placed on every one of Your children. I will walk in that truth today, knowing that You desire my time to be marked with intentionality rather than busyness. In Jesus's name, amen.

THE POWER OF OUR POTENTIAL

I pray that your hearts will be flooded with light so that you can understand the confident hope He has given to those He called—His holy people who are His rich and glorious inheritance.

EPHESIANS 1:18 NLT

Do we truly understand the depth of our potential?

Even on our best days, we often place limits on ourselves. We shrink to fit the version of life we think we can manage. We hold on to comfort, even when we long to step into the impossible. We say we want to believe God for big things, but hope they'll come in ways that don't stretch us too far. We want the adventure without the unknown. The calling without the cost. The purpose without the pruning.

But Scripture says, "Your hearts will be flooded with light so that you can understand the confident hope . . ." (Ephesians 1:18 NLT). It's His light—His truth—that awakens our hearts to what's really possible. And once His light floods in, we begin to see ourselves not through the lens of insecurity or past mistakes, but through the eyes of the One who made us.

This isn't about unlocking some hidden version of ourselves for applause or achievement. It's about becoming more like Jesus. Because your true potential? It's not measured by success, but by surrender. And it's already been seen, known, and called out by the One who gave you breath.

day 3

What might be holding you back from reaching your potential?

Dear God, thank You for being a sure and loving Father. You believe in me, and You desire to use me in mighty ways. Help me break out of my socially acceptable box and run hard after You. In Jesus's name, amen.

HE KNOWS LIFE IS A LOT

Truly my soul finds rest in God;
my salvation comes from Him.
PSALM 62:1 NIV

"Unclench your jaw. Take your tongue off the roof of your mouth. Relax your hands." The instructor's words caught me off guard. Wait . . . was I doing all of that? Turns out—I was. And I didn't even know it.

It's surprising how often our bodies carry tension we never meant to hold. But isn't that true of our lives too? We live clenched. Braced. On guard. Not because we consciously choose it, but because the rhythm of our culture rewards constant motion and quiet pressure. We hold tight—physically and emotionally—without even realizing it. But that kind of tension takes a toll. It dulls our awareness. It wears on our joy. It keeps our souls in a subtle state of defense.

And yet, the invitation of Jesus is not to sprint harder. It's to rest. To breathe. To remember that nothing in your hands is worth more than the hope in your heart. So maybe today, you pause. Unclench your jaw. Let your shoulders drop. Open your hands—both physically and spiritually—and just be. Be with the One who isn't asking you to prove anything, but instead is simply inviting you to be present.

day 4

Write a note to tell yourself to relax your jaw and unclench your hands.

Dear Jesus, thank You for Your peace. Help me to be thankful for the blessings and the burdens I have, trusting that You are my Help and Provider. I am not crazy; I am human, and You love me more than anything. In Jesus's name, amen.

RED LIGHT, GREEN LIGHT

The Lord is not slow in keeping His promise,
as some understand slowness. Instead He is patient with you,
not wanting anyone to perish, but everyone to come to repentance.
II PETER 3:9 NIV

Remember the childhood game Red Light, Green Light? Everyone stands in a line, and when the leader calls out, "Green light," everyone runs forward with everything they've got. When they yell, "Red light," everyone freezes. The goal is simple: be the first to reach the front. But the catch? If you're still moving when the red light is called, you're out. The desire to win becomes so strong, we often compromise our ability to listen to the voice giving direction.

Isn't that a picture of life sometimes? We want to move forward, gain ground, reach the next milestone—so much so that we miss the cues from the One holding the signal. But what if God's voice doesn't match the world's rhythm? He might say, "Green light," when the world says, "Stop," and "Red light," when everything in us wants to go. Why? Because He knows when we need rest. He knows we weren't made to compete, but to trust. The race isn't against others—it's a walk with Him.

So today, let's tune in to His signals. Let stillness be a gift. Let it restore your soul, refuel your spirit, and ready your heart for whatever green light comes next.

day 5

In what areas of your life has God given you a "red light"? What can you learn from pausing instead of moving forward?

Dear Jesus, thank You for being a God of peace with perfect timeliness and patience. I trust Your direction even when it looks different from what I was expecting. Help me to lean into stillness and take a deep breath. In Jesus's name, amen.

JUST PASSING THROUGH

For we know that if the tent that is our earthly home is destroyed, we have a building from God, a house not made with hands, eternal in the heavens.
II CORINTHIANS 5:1 ESV

The more life we experience, the more we learn that grief wears many faces. It can arrive at any moment. It spares no one, often bringing us to our knees before we even realize what's happening.

We cry out, "Lord, where are You? Why?" We scan the possibilities, wondering why this had to unfold the way it did. Life, as we knew it, shifts. While the loss of a loved one, a divorce, or financial devastation are easy to name as grief, other losses aren't as obvious. Sometimes grief looks like releasing the timeline we'd hoped for, letting go of a relationship that's become unhealthy, or facing consequences we brought upon ourselves. We often mislabel grief, not realizing the ache that's settled into the empty spaces. But even in our confusion, the soul recognizes desperation. It wakes us up to the truth: life on earth will leave its mark in knee-prints.

When pain becomes real, we begin to understand—Jesus is our only constant. As we cry out in prayer, He doesn't always give immediate answers, but He always gives something deeper: Himself. And in those sacred exchanges, our hands find His again—linked, held, and never letting go.

day 6

In what ways are you feeling grief in this season of life?

Dear Jesus, thank You that You are always near, even when my heart is weary or sad. Will You remind me of my forever home? Let the truth of eternity with You permeate my heart with hope and joy. In Jesus's name, amen.

POSTURE OF PEACE

You will keep in perfect peace those whose minds are steadfast, because they trust in You.
ISAIAH 26:3 NIV

Have you ever met someone who seemed to carry a supernatural calm—even when life threw them curveballs? No warning. No preparation. And yet they didn't lose their peace or let go of hope. Chances are, someone comes to mind. We admire their steadiness. Maybe even envy it. Deep down, we find ourselves whispering, "Lord, I want whatever that is."

Of all the things we chase in this life, there is nothing more valuable than peace. It's what we're really after beneath all the striving and achieving. We want to wake up with joy, live with contentment, and trust that our heavenly Father is as faithful as He says He is. We long to be people of peace—especially when life feels anything but peaceful.

But peace isn't passive. It's a choice. A posture. Choosing peace doesn't mean avoiding hardship; it means anchoring ourselves in the truth that God is with us in it. As Philippians 4:7 reminds us, His peace "surpasses all understanding" (ESV). It quiets fear, steadies chaos, and reminds us that we don't face anything alone.

True peace isn't found in a perfect life—it's found in a present God.

day 7

How will you decide to take a posture of peace today?

Dear Jesus, thank You for the richest gift I could ever ask for in this life—Your peace. When I begin to feel pressured or worried, recalibrate my mind. In Jesus's name, amen.

EVEN THE WAVES OBEY HIM

He replied, "You of little faith, why are you so afraid?"
Then He got up and rebuked the winds and the waves,
and it was completely calm. The men were amazed and asked,
"What kind of man is this? Even the winds and the waves obey Him!"
MATTHEW 8:26–27 NIV

Close your eyes and picture the ocean—vast, unrelenting, full of beauty and danger all at once. Most of us know what it feels like to misjudge its strength—to be knocked over by a wave we didn't see coming, pulled by a current we couldn't fight.

That's the kind of sea the disciples were in—Matthew 8:18–27—when the storm surrounded their boat like a clenched fist. Chaos above, chaos below. And Jesus? Asleep. It feels offensive at first—how can He rest when we're drowning?

But when they woke Him, He didn't rebuke them—He rebuked the waves. Because sometimes the storm outside just reveals the storm within. And Jesus knew they needed more than calm seas—they needed the kind of faith that anchors in Him, not in outcomes.

His presence wasn't absent; it was just unshaken. That same Jesus—the One who told the wind to hush and the sea to still—is in your boat too. So, when your world spins sideways and the waves come fast, remember: The One who made the sea is your shelter. And your peace is not up for negotiation—it's protected by the Prince of it.

day 8

Remember a time when Jesus calmed a storm in your life. Do you believe He will do it again?

Dear Jesus, thank You for telling me of the time You stilled the waves and calmed the storm. Remind my heart that You are my safe place, the Source of my peace. In Jesus's name, amen.

KNOWING THE HOPE GIVER

May the God of hope fill you with
all joy and peace as you trust in Him,
so that you may overflow with hope
by the power of the Holy Spirit.
ROMANS 15:13 NIV

We often think that if we could just shift our perspective, everything would fall into place. And yes—perspective is powerful. But sometimes we get so focused on trying to see differently, we forget to trust the One who sees it all.

What if the breakthrough isn't found in finding new glasses—but in fixing our eyes on the Guide? What if the miracle isn't a detour or shortcut, but learning to follow the steady Hand that never leads us astray? This journey isn't a maze we have to figure out; it's a map He's already drawn. And our security comes not from knowing every turn, but from knowing who's walking us through it.

God doesn't hold hope behind glass, dishing it out like a reward for good behavior. He doesn't ration peace based on performance. No—He is lavish with His love, generous in His guidance, and eager for us to know His heart.

When the Giver becomes the goal, clarity follows. And when we walk with the One who holds the map, we don't have to fear where we're headed. Even in the dark, our steps can be sure—because the One leading us never loses His way.

day 9

Do you trust God to guide you? Why or why not?

Lord, thank You for being the Giver of all hope. Let me draw near, spend time with You, and be reassured that because I can trust Your heart, I can always have hope beyond my situations. In Jesus's name, amen.

CHANGE OF PACE

"Consider the lilies, how they grow: they neither toil nor spin, yet I tell you,
even Solomon in all his glory was not arrayed like one of these.
But if God so clothes the grass, which is alive in the field today,
and tomorrow is thrown into the oven, how much more
will he clothe you, O you of little faith!"

LUKE 12:27–28 ESV

Our bodies are strengthened by resistance. Muscle growth depends on it—without tension, there's no transformation. But we often forget: our souls need resistance too.

In the physical world, we change our workouts to see results. In the spiritual life, the same principle applies. Yet culture insists we stay in motion—always doing, proving, achieving. Stillness becomes a luxury we feel guilty for craving. But what if slowing down wasn't weakness? What if rest wasn't an interruption, but an invitation?

There will be resistance. The world may not understand your pause. Even your own mind might fight it. But growth rarely happens at breakneck speed—it happens in surrender. Jesus never asked us to move faster than peace can follow. He modeled rhythms of withdrawal, of prayer, of quiet. And when we match His pace, we begin to hear Him more clearly. Eventually, the chaos around us loses its grip on the chaos within us. Because when you walk with the One who sets the tempo, you stop racing toward a life He already promised—you start receiving it instead.

day 10

What are the advantages of slowing down?
What steps will you take today to slow down?

Jesus, thank You for the ability to slow down and be still in You. Settle my mind when I feel the pressure to speed up and remind me that You are transforming me. In Jesus's name, amen.

NOT THE WORLD'S HOPE

But those who hope in the LORD will renew their strength.
They will soar on wings like eagles;
they will run and not grow weary,
they will walk and not be faint.
ISAIAH 40:31 NIV

You've probably heard it or said it yourself: "I hope it all works out!" It sounds optimistic, even faithful. But more often than not, that kind of hope is just wishful thinking dressed in polite words—a desire for something good, without the confidence that it will come. But biblical hope? It's an entirely different thing.

Biblical hope is not a fingers-crossed feeling—it's confident expectation. It's anchored in the unchanging character of God, not in the unpredictability of our circumstances. When we say, "I hope in God," we're not wondering if He'll come through. We're declaring that He already has, and He always will—just as He said. This kind of hope reshapes how we walk. We stop chasing outcomes and start trusting the One who holds them. We stop comparing our pace to others and start receiving strength for our own race. We stop bracing for disappointment and start leaning into divine assurance.

Hope in God is not fragile—it's fiercely grounded. It is rest for the restless, renewal for the worn out, and direction for the one who forgot which way was forward. And when hope is planted in Him, it never stops growing.

What are some practical ways you can rely on God today?

Dear Jesus, thank You that Your hope is not one that diminishes or discourages me. Show me how to cling to Your hope. In Jesus's name, amen.

RETURN TO THE RESERVOIR

"He who believes in Me, as the Scripture said,
'From his innermost being will flow rivers of living water.'"
JOHN 7:38 NASB1995

What does faith have to do with a reservoir? A reservoir stores water that sustains life when drought hits. When rivers run dry, the reservoir supplies what's missing—quietly, steadily, dependably. And our souls? They need a reservoir too.

Because dry seasons will come. Loneliness, disappointment, silence, waiting. And when they do, if we don't have a deep supply of hope built up, our view of God gets distorted by the dust around us. That's why faith matters. It's not about pretending the wilderness doesn't exist—it's about having somewhere to draw from when it does.

When your reservoir is full of His promises, His teachings, and His presence, you can draw strength when your emotions can't carry you. You can resist retaliation, choose self-control, and pause before letting discouragement speak for you. Instead of reacting from lack, you respond from overflow.

And where do we fill that reservoir? Only at the well of Living Water. Not performance. Not positivity. Just Jesus—our Source of wholeness and wellness. So visit the well often. Drink deeply. Store up the truth that will carry you when life feels dry. He doesn't just meet us in the wilderness—He sustains us through it.

day 12

Have you been turning to God to get filled up? If not, what is stopping you? If so, in what ways has God been filling you up lately?

Lord, thank You that You are the well that never runs dry. Thank You for being my reservoir, dependable and abundant in all You give. In Jesus's name, amen.

KNEELING IN NEED

Come, let us worship and bow down,
let us kneel before the LORD our Maker.
PSALM 95:6 NASB1995

Kneeling is one of the clearest pictures of surrender. It's the posture of yielded authority, of humility in motion. And while we might like to believe we live bowed low before God, we often only find ourselves on our knees when we've run out of strength to stand.

God knows this about us. He formed us, fully aware of our tendency to strive, grip tightly, and delay surrender until we're depleted or undone. But even then—especially then—He meets us. The ground may feel like rock bottom, but to God, it's holy ground.

Because kneeling isn't weakness. It's alignment. It's choosing the posture we were always meant to live from—dependent, openhanded, and fully aware of our need for Him. And when we kneel, He draws near. Not with shame or silence, but with comfort and clarity. He lifts our chin, breathes life into our weary places, and reminds us that surrender is where hope begins.

Prayer isn't just communication—it's connection. Whether we're speaking or silently aching, kneeling puts our hearts in the position where heaven moves and peace floods in. And some of the most powerful things God does begin when we simply bend low.

day 13

Spend fifteen minutes in prayer today (or fifteen minutes more than you normally would). Afterward, write about your experience. If you didn't have words, describe the thoughts or feelings you had while being still and waiting for God.

Dear Jesus, thank You that nothing is too big or too small to bring to Your feet. You desire more than anything for me to stop and kneel so that I can be reminded of who You are and who I am in You. In Jesus's name, amen.

FIOS: FIGURE-IT-OUT SYNDROME

And I am sure of this, that he who began a good work in you will bring it to completion at the day of Jesus Christ.
PHILIPPIANS 1:6 ESV

Patience sounds great—until it means waiting on something we deeply desire. Waiting for clarity. Waiting for healing. Waiting for a breakthrough that feels long overdue. Suddenly, patience doesn't feel peaceful—it feels painful.

We live in a fix-it culture. We've been taught that if we just try hard enough, think long enough, or worry intensely enough, we'll find the solution. But most of life's deeper questions can't be solved through striving.

What if the goal isn't solving the problem—but surrendering it? The moment we release our grip and stop playing fixer, we begin to experience real peace. Not because the problem disappears, but because we finally hand it to the One who never asks us to carry what He already claimed. God didn't create your mind so that it could outrun His timing. He didn't craft your soul to hold what only He can heal.

Instead, we can replace F.I.O.S. with *F.I.O.J.—Figure It Out, Jesus.* That's the abundant life. Not the one where everything is solved, but the one where everything is surrendered. And the best part? He always figures it out.

day 14

What are some areas in your life in which you're holding on to control? How could surrendering those areas bring you peace?

Dear Jesus, thank You for being the solution to every problem I encounter. I surrender the desire to figure it all out because I know that You are trustworthy and faithful. In Jesus's name, amen.

VULNERABILITY WITHOUT PITY

But to the degree that you share the sufferings of Christ,
keep on rejoicing, so that also at the revelation
of His glory you may rejoice with exultation.
I PETER 4:13 NASB1995

Authenticity may feel trendy—but real vulnerability isn't about performance or polish. True vulnerability is sacred space—a heart exposed not for applause, but for connection, healing, and truth.

Platforms like Instagram have made it easier to pull back the curtain, to let others see the mess beneath the filter. And that's a beautiful thing. The "grace over perfection" message is needed more than ever. Because what we hide, we begin to believe is shameful. But what we bring into the light? God redeems and redefines.

Still, vulnerability isn't the destination—it's the doorway. It begins with honesty but leads us toward wholeness. After we cry together, let's heal together. Let's remind each other that vulnerability is not weakness—it's evidence of courage, proof that we know where our hope comes from and why it holds.

We don't stay exposed for pity—we open up so light can flood in. And through that light, we gain strength, community, resilience, and spiritual authority. We don't just survive our struggles—we stand in victory through them. Together.

day 15

What are you afraid will happen if you are authentic with others? Think about someone you trust—whether a friend or family member. How could you practice being more vulnerable with them? What would that look like for you?

Dear Jesus, thank You for giving me the courage and the strength to show up and be vulnerable with others. Help me to remember that You expose weakness so it can be made stronger. In Jesus's name, amen.

A STEEL-LIKE HOPE

But this I call to mind, and therefore I have hope:
The steadfast love of the LORD never ceases;
his mercies never come to an end; they are new
every morning; great is your faithfulness.
LAMENTATIONS 3:21–23 ESV

We've all witnessed it—that quiet strength in someone whose life doesn't make sense on paper. You know their story. You've seen the loss they've endured, the battles they're still fighting. And yet, their joy remains steady. Their posture is peaceful. Their hope doesn't seem to match their circumstances—and that's exactly the point. There's something unshakable about a person whose confidence isn't tethered to outcomes. The diagnosis may still be uncertain. The finances may still be tight. The family strain may still linger. And yet, they don't crumble. Why? Because their hope isn't circumstantial. It's rooted. It's steel-like—refined in fire, but not scorched by it.

So we ask ourselves: Where is our hope anchored? Does it rise and fall with headlines, phone calls, or shifting seasons? Or is it fixed on the One who wastes nothing—not even hardship?

Hope isn't a feeling to chase. It's a reality we choose. It's a declaration that even here, even now, God is good, God is near, and God is working. When we live from that place, our lives become sermons. And the kind of hope that holds up under pressure? That's the kind that helps others rise too.

day 16

What stops you from trusting God more? Be honest.

Dear Jesus, thank You for the gift of hope. No matter where I am or what I face, the assurance of Your provision and love will guide me forward. May my countenance, perspective, and posture reflect my hope in You. In Jesus's name, amen.

EXPECTATIONS FROM THE GARDEN

This God—his way is perfect; the word of the LORD proves true; he is a shield for all those who take refuge in him.

II SAMUEL 22:31 ESV

The Garden of Eden was the picture of perfection—wholeness untouched by pain, disappointment, or shame. No striving. No regret. Adam and Eve walked in full unity with God, completely exposed yet completely safe. There wasn't a single worry in the world—literally. And though we don't live in Eden, we carry an ache for it. Somewhere deep in our hearts is a memory of what was meant to be—perfection, peace, permanence. So, it makes sense that we expect a lot from people, from ourselves, from life.

But the problem is not the desire for good—it's where we place our hope. If we place our expectations on people with Eden-sized weight, they will inevitably crumble. We'll feel discontented, disappointed, and discouraged—not because they failed, but because we were asking them to be something only Jesus can be. Perfection is not the standard—we already have a Savior. And He doesn't call us to perform; He calls us to trust.

When we remember that only Jesus can carry the weight of our hope, we begin to live with grace—for ourselves, for others, and for the messiness in between. And in that place, hope doesn't disappoint—it anchors. Every time.

day 17

What are some things in your life that you're still hoping will be perfect, even though you know only Jesus can truly fulfill that desire? Write about what those things are and why they're hard to let go of.

Dear Jesus, thank You for making me in Your image, bearing perfection and honor. Help me rely on You and give grace to others. Thank You for loving me. In Jesus's name, amen.

PRAYER PAVES THE WAY

"Therefore I tell you, whatever you ask for in prayer, believe that you have received it, and it will be yours."
MARK 11:24 NIV

Remember the arcade claw machine—the one where you drop a metal claw into a sea of stuffed animals, hoping to come up lucky? Occasionally, it delivers. But most of the time, the claw fumbles, grabs too loosely, or drops the prize just before victory.

Sometimes we treat prayer like that—as an unpredictable gamble. We invest time, whisper our hopes, and then brace ourselves for disappointment. We're not always sure it works. But prayer was never meant to be a claw-in-the-dark shot at hope. Prayer is a sacred lifeline—a consistent, powerful connection to the God who sees all, knows all, and cares deeply. Scripture tells us to pray without ceasing, to pray when we're tempted, to devote ourselves to prayer. Not because it's a religious duty, but because it realigns our heart with the One who holds all things together. Prayer isn't about getting perfect results; it's about practicing perfect surrender. It's our soul's way of remembering who is truly in control—and whom we belong to.

Every time we pray, we pave a path for peace, for perspective, and for God's presence to meet us in the middle of it all. And He always does.

day 18

What have you stopped praying about because you haven't received an answer? Would you consider praying about it again today? Maybe even writing out your prayer in the lines below?

Dear Jesus, thank You for the opportunity to be in constant conversation with You. Help me to seek Your guidance and wisdom before all else. In Jesus's name, amen.

REMOVE THE SCARLET LETTER

But the Lord God helps me;
therefore I have not been disgraced;
therefore I have set my face like a flint,
and I know that I shall not be put to shame.
ISAIAH 50:7 ESV

We all have chapters we'd rather skip—messy stories, broken places, seasons filled with confusion, fear, and regret. Pages that hold the version of ourselves we hope no one ever sees. And yet we often live as if those old stories are still our identity. We carry invisible scarlet letters—self-assigned labels of shame, failure, or guilt—quietly believing they disqualify us from joy, freedom, or purpose. But Jesus never called us to erase our past. He came to redeem it.

Your history isn't a source of shame—it's the soil from which compassion, humility, and deep understanding have grown. When we believe in the redemptive power of Jesus, we're not just saying He forgives us—we're declaring that He uses every part of us, even the hardest parts, to build something beautiful.

Your past prepared your heart for this very moment. It shaped your empathy. It refined your calling. And it magnified your need for grace, which only deepens your gratitude for it now. You are not defined by who you were. You are defined by the One who made you new. So let go of the label. You've been covered in grace—and He calls you whole.

day 19

What areas of your past do you feel need His transformation?

Dear Jesus, thank You for taking all my guilt and my shame upon the cross. I know that Your redemptive power turns even my biggest failures into springboards for greatness. In Jesus's name, amen.

STILLNESS INVITES THE PROMPTING

"When the Spirit of truth comes, he will guide you into all the truth, for he will not speak on his own authority, but whatever he hears he will speak, and he will declare to you the things that are to come."
JOHN 16:13 ESV

Remember being a kid, convinced you weren't tired—until your head hit the pillow and sleep swept in like a wave? Or those quiet times at church camp when journaling felt forced—until pens were suddenly going a million miles an hour, scribbling what hearts had been holding all along?

Stillness makes room for what noise keeps buried. Like a child finally resting, stillness invites what God has been waiting to release. Not because He's been silent, but because we've been scattered. He doesn't force His way through our chaos—He gently waits for us to pause.

We often don't know what we truly need. But He does. Stillness is a holy interruption—a reset that grounds us in truth and anchors us in His presence. It slows our striving and opens our spirit to receive the wisdom we didn't even know we were missing.

It's not that we're deaf or He's distant. It's that we've filled every crevice of our day with noise, then wondered why we couldn't hear Him. But when we stop, even briefly, the clutter quiets, the Spirit stirs, and we remember: He's not withholding. He's whispering.
And the prompting always follows the pause.

day 20

Commit to fifteen minutes of stillness today and write down what you felt about the experience afterward.

Dear Jesus, thank You for the way You faithfully show up when I make time for You. Help me to create this time of stillness and allow my spirit to be prompted. In Jesus's name, amen.

LIVING ON AUTOPILOT

Look carefully then how you walk,
not as unwise but as wise,
making the best use of the time,
because the days are evil.
EPHESIANS 5:15–16 ESV

We've all done it—pulled into a driveway or parking lot and suddenly realized we can't remember how we got there. We stopped at lights, took turns, shifted gears . . . but it all happened without much thought. The autopilot took over.

How often do we move through life the same way? We keep driving, keep doing, keep going—without ever checking if we're headed where we actually want to be. The work feels hard, the path unclear, and we wonder why our hope feels thin. But we haven't paused long enough to invite God into the route.

Autopilot may keep us moving, but it won't keep us aligned. And just because the desire is there doesn't mean the direction is right. If we want to live awake, we need more than momentum—we need His presence. Jesus is ready to renew your mind and steady your soul. But He doesn't force His way behind the wheel—He waits for your surrender. He waits to guide. It starts with stillness, with choosing truth and releasing control.

You don't have to keep coasting or living to survive. When you hand Him the wheel, you'll find He's been ready to lead you all along.

day 21

What routines have you been going through without much thought or awareness? Reflect on why you think this has been happening and how it might be affecting your relationship with God or others.

Dear Jesus, thank You for the way You lead me, even when my pride or fear has kept me from seeking You. Turn off the music, shut off my distractions, remove "autopilot" mode, and let me be alert as I seek Your will. In Jesus's name, amen.

WHEN GOD IS SILENT IN OUR STILLNESS

"Blessed are those who hunger and thirst
for righteousness, for they shall be satisfied."
MATTHEW 5:6 ESV

We've all been there—seeking God's guidance, laying bare our hearts in prayer, only to be met with silence. We wait, watching the heavens, and wonder if He's gone quiet on the very thing He once invited us to bring before Him. The urgency in our souls aches for a response, but the stillness feels endless.

Why would a loving God be silent? Not because He lacks answers. Not because your situation is too complicated or your past too messy. The reality is, many times He's already spoken to us through His Word. Before we assume He's absent, we must ask: Have we sought His truth in Scripture? Have we given space for what He's already said to settle in?

Other times, His silence simply is. He is God. And while we may crave explanations, He is not obligated to provide them. His quiet is not a punishment or neglect—it's often an invitation.

When the air feels empty, don't run toward noise. Resist the urge to fill the gap with lesser voices. His silence may be sacred space—a holy hush calling you deeper, beneath the surface, into stillness where trust is formed and faith matures.

day 22

What thoughts or feelings come up when you experience silence from God? Reflect on how you respond to times when you feel distant from Him and what you think He might be trying to teach you during those moments.

Dear Jesus, thank You for always answering in the most perfect way, even when that feels like absence to me. You are God alone, and I trust Your ways. In Jesus's name, amen.

DISCOVERING OUR PURPOSE

Many are the plans in a person's heart,
but it is the LORD's purpose that prevails.
PROVERBS 19:21 NIV

Purpose—it's a word we hear constantly, but when pressed for a definition, most of us fumble. Culture often ties it to productivity, platform, or performance. We ask: *What are my hands building? How are my days being spent?* And if we can't point to clear results, we wonder if we've missed it entirely.

But God's view of purpose isn't rooted in visibility—it's rooted in transformation. He cares deeply about what we do, but even more about who we're becoming. Our truest calling is to look more like Jesus—moment by moment, thought by thought, layer by layer.

Purpose unfolds not in striving but in surrender. When we slow down and sync our pace with His, our lives begin to take shape—not by what the world deems successful, but by the quiet, steady work He's doing in our hearts. Stillness tunes our ears to His voice, and when we listen, we hear His gentle guidance: "A little to the right . . . there you go." Suddenly, we're not chasing purpose—we're walking with the One who defines it.

Your purpose isn't a far-off arrival. It's a daily alignment. And when you're walking with Him, you're already in it.

day 23

Who are you becoming?

What is God doing to test your heart right now?

Lord, thank You for molding me, transforming me, and using me according to Your purposes. Renew my mind when I begin to define my worth by what my hands are doing, and recalibrate me to the truth. In Jesus's name, amen.

WHAT'S YOUR NAME AGAIN?

Having purified your souls by your obedience
to the truth for a sincere brotherly love,
love one another earnestly from a pure heart.
I PETER 1:22 ESV

Remembering someone's name might seem like a small thing—but to the person being remembered, it can mean everything. Names tether us to identity. They say, *You matter. I see you.* And yet, in our fast-paced culture, we brush past this simple gift. We half-listen, convince ourselves we'll check later on social media, and move on.

But did Jesus ever forget a name? Ever treat someone like a blur in the background? No—names mattered to Him. He called people out personally, intentionally, lovingly. And He still does. Remembering a name may feel minor, but it's one of the most powerful ways to communicate dignity in a world full of distractions. It tells someone they're not overlooked, not invisible, not just passing through.

When we slow down and spend time with Jesus, He doesn't just still our racing thoughts—He sharpens our vision for others. Stillness makes us more present. It awakens compassion. It helps us ask better questions and stick around long enough to truly hear the answers.

So, what if we started seeing names not as details to recall, but as doorways to deeper love? Because sometimes, remembering a name is the first step to reflecting His heart.

day 24

Are there distractions, internal thoughts, or emotions that pull your focus away? Reflect on how these barriers affect your relationships and how you might practice being more present when others are speaking.

Lord, thank You for helping me to be still in You so that I can better understand how to love those around me. Give me eyes to see their needs, willing hands to help them, and an obedient spirit that does not question the appointments You put in my path. In Jesus's name, amen.

AN IDENTITY ISSUE

But you are a chosen people, a royal priesthood,
a holy nation, God's special possession,
that you may declare the praises of Him
who called you out of darkness into His wonderful light.
I PETER 2:9 NIV

Why is stillness so hard to practice? Why do we feel the need to be everything to everyone, everywhere, all at once? Deep down, do we truly desire this frantic pace? The need to overextend, overachieve, and overplease often comes from one root: we're chasing affirmation. We want others to see our value, because somewhere along the way, we stopped seeing it in ourselves.

But identity was never something we were meant to earn—it's something we're invited to receive. God saw every one of our flaws and failures and still chose the cross. Our worth isn't up for debate—it was decided on Calvary. We are not defined by our performance, but by His finished work. When we live from that truth, the lies become easier to spot: That pressure? That shame? That voice of inadequacy? It's not from Jesus. In stillness, we learn to detect deception, reject it, and replace it with the unshakable truth of who we are in Christ. Our identity becomes rooted, not reactive—anchored in grace, not striving.

You don't have to prove what's already been purchased. Your identity is secure. And living from that place? That's where real purpose begins.

day 25

Whom are you seeking validation from,
and why do you think their approval matters to you?
What does it feel like when you receive validation from them,
and how does it affect your sense of self-worth? Consider what it
would look like to seek your value and identity in God instead.

Dear Jesus, thank You for weaving me perfectly in Your image. When I find my mind wandering or letting my identity be up for negotiation, take me back to Your Word and the truth that sets me free. In Jesus's name, amen.

LONG STORY SHORT, PLEASE

God did this so that they would seek Him and perhaps reach out for Him and find Him, though He is not far from any one of us.

ACTS 17:27 NIV

Have you ever noticed how little patience we have for the whole story? We crave the condensed version—just the highlights, the climax, and the conclusion, all packaged neatly for quick consumption. No waiting, no wrestling. Just answers.

This craving for instant insight has made us deeply uncomfortable with process. We'd rather scroll for inspiration than sit still for transformation. We gather facts about God, but bypass time with God. We can memorize Scripture, quote truth, and fill our minds with knowledge. But until we spend time lingering in His presence—worshiping, listening, receiving—we will always feel disconnected from what we claim to believe. There truly is no shortcut for intimacy with Him.

The long story short is this: there is no long story short. Spiritual depth isn't downloaded; it's cultivated. Faith grows in slow soil, watered by surrender and steadied by grace. There's no bullet-point version of transformation. No outline that replaces obedience. Just a real relationship—formed moment by moment in the quiet presence of our tender, teaching Father.

Don't rush the story. The fullness of God is revealed not just in the ending—but in every chapter where He meets you along the way.

day 26

How could you incorporate worship into your day beyond traditional moments of prayer or music? Reflect on the different ways worship can be expressed—through your actions, your thoughts, your interactions with others, or even your work.

Jesus, thank You for desiring to know me intimately and personally. Help me seek You, desire more of You, and make being with You a necessary part of my everyday life. In Jesus's name, amen.

LETTING THE DIRT FALL

The unfolding of your words gives light;
it imparts understanding to the simple.
PSALM 119:130 ESV

Mindfulness may be a trending topic, but the struggle behind it is ancient—staying present in a world that constantly pulls us in a thousand directions. We want stillness, but even our reminders to pause get interrupted by calls, notifications, or calendar alerts. We set out to sit with Jesus, but life barges in. Needs arise. And suddenly the line between "urgent" and "important" blurs, and our peace feels hijacked.

But something sacred happens when we stay—when we sit longer than feels natural, when we refuse to rush away. It's in that holy stillness that the dirt in our minds begins to settle and the water clears. Truth rises. Perspective sharpens. We begin to see ourselves not through the lens of chaos, but through the eyes of Christ. His voice helps us distinguish distraction from destiny. We stop reacting and start discerning.

Stillness isn't passive—it's purifying. It sifts the noise, exposes what's real, and anchors us in the light of His Word. So sit . . . then sit some more. Let the dirt fall. Because while you're waiting, He's working. And what He's refining in the quiet will change how you live in the noise.

day 27

In what ways has the "urgent" knocked out the "important" in your life? What have you sacrificed or put on the back burner because of urgency, and how has that impacted your peace or sense of purpose? Consider what changes you might make to reorder your priorities and give more attention to the important things that have been overlooked.

Jesus, thank You for the invitation to sit and be still with You. Help me prioritize this, remembering that all else in my life will sort itself out when I give You my focus. In Jesus's name, amen.

LOVING LIKE JESUS DOES

"This is my commandment, that you love one another as I have loved you. Greater love has no one than this, that someone lay down his life for his friends. You are my friends if you do what I command you."

JOHN 15:12–14 ESV

It's surprisingly easy to shift from love to frustration. One unmet expectation, a careless comment, or a moment of exclusion—and suddenly, our affection feels conditional. We long to love like Jesus, yet we often love like humans: responsive, reactive, and self-protective.

But what if love didn't hinge on being treated right? What if our response wasn't retaliation, but release? What if, instead of holding grudges or rehearsing what they did wrong, we chose to love anyway? Not because it's easy. But because we've been loved like that first.

Jesus calls us to love not from a place of emptiness, but from the overflow of being deeply loved by Him. That kind of love isn't weak—it's brave. It doesn't ignore the pain, but it refuses to let pain be the final word. When we anchor our identity in Christ's unwavering love, we stop grasping for affirmation and start offering grace. Our hearts become less about self-protection and more about Spirit-led presence.

Loving like Jesus doesn't mean we won't feel hurt—but it does mean we're no longer ruled by it. And in a world that withholds love, there's nothing more radical than someone who keeps giving it away.

day 28

Is there someone in your life you're struggling to forgive? Take a moment to write about the situation and why it feels difficult to let go. Then reflect on what it might look like to offer love freely—even when it's hard.

Dear Jesus, thank You for loving me beyond what I can ever fathom or deserve. Remind my heart to not take things personally and to love others the way You love me. In Jesus's name, amen.

PRACTICE PAUSING

The LORD is good to those who wait for him,
to the soul who seeks him.
LAMENTATIONS 3:25 ESV

The Apple Watch is pretty impressive. It tracks patterns, prompts movement, and even reminds you to breathe. But what surprised me most? How much it revealed about my rhythm. I was staying up too late, skipping early movement, and wondering why my days felt misaligned.

Once I began adjusting my habits—more rest, more intention, more margin—everything shifted. It wasn't just about sleep or exercise. It was about space for renewal. The prompts to pause throughout the day, once dismissed as unnecessary, began showing up at just the right time—divine interruptions in disguise. And isn't that how God works too?

Pausing feels counterintuitive in a world that worships hustle. Stillness seems wasteful when to-do lists scream for attention. But carving out time for silence isn't childish—it's courageous. It reorients us. It allows us to give God room to speak. And sometimes, that's exactly why we avoid it—because deep down, we know He will. Stillness reveals. And revelation, though beautiful, can be uncomfortable. But the invitation remains: Slow down. Breathe. Be still. Your soul doesn't need more speed. It needs more surrender, more presence, and more of Him.

day 29

If you allowed yourself to pause today—truly stop, even just for a moment—what fears or worries would come up for you? What do you think might happen if you stopped being busy or productive? Where do those fears come from, and are they rooted in past experiences or current pressures?

Dear Jesus, thank You for being present at all times. Today, I choose to pause and notice Your presence and provision. In Jesus's name, amen.

NO TIME FOR RESENTMENT

"Fear not, for you will not be put to shame;
and do not feel humiliated, for you will not be disgraced;
but you will forget the shame of your youth,
and the reproach of your widowhood you will remember no more."
ISAIAH 54:4 NASB1995

The moment we set a new goal, discouragement often sneaks in. Isn't it strange how quickly we can sabotage our own resolutions? We want change, but the second we commit to growth, resistance rises. When we begin shifting our mindset or stepping toward healing, the pressure intensifies. Old habits whisper lies. Unexpected obstacles surface. Shame from our past tries to steal the hope of a better future and distort our vision of who God says we are.

But we are not powerless. We don't have time for resentment—because we're too busy fixing our eyes on the One who redeems. The enemy may want to derail our progress, but God has already declared our identity: chosen, equipped, known, and set apart. There's no room for bitterness when praise fills the air. We're not anchored in outcomes—we're anchored in Jesus. Our eyes carry light because we belong to the Light of the World. And wherever we go, that light goes too.

So today, throw off what entangles. Release the weight that's not yours to carry. You were never called to stay stuck in regret. You were called to run free, fueled by grace and focused on glory.

day 30

When you think about creating meaningful change in your life, what comes to mind? Are there things that feel like obstacles—or are you feeling ready and clear? What supports your growth, and what slows it down? How do you respond to the idea of change: with excitement, fear, resistance, or hope?

Dear Jesus, thank You for offering me a clean slate with every day that passes. Your grace really is more than enough. In Jesus's name, amen.

DON'T BORROW FROM TOMORROW

"Therefore do not worry about tomorrow,
for tomorrow will worry about itself.
Each day has enough trouble of its own."
MATTHEW 6:34 NIV

There it goes again—our minds reaching ahead. Our hands are already full with today's responsibilities, yet we stretch toward the jar of tomorrow. *What's in there?* we wonder. *Will I be ready for it?* we worry. So we speculate. Predict. Plan. We try to build a safety net from guesswork, gathering emotional reserves just in case. But in the process, we trade today's peace for tomorrow's unknowns.

Here's the truth: Grief will come. Disappointment will find us. Rejection may ring the doorbell, and hardship might pull up a chair. But when those moments arrive, God will meet us there, just as He is meeting us here. His mercies aren't stored in the future—they're new every morning, tailored for the day at hand.

Grabbing tomorrow steals from what God is offering us now. But when we stay in today's grace, we travel lighter. We stop carrying bags we were never meant to hold. We stop needing all the answers to experience peace. You don't need to forecast the future to walk in faith. You need to trust the One who already holds it.

So, unclench your hands. Stay present. And let Jesus carry what only He can.

day 31

In what ways does worry influence your choices or your outlook on life? What might shift if you let go of the constant "what-ifs" and simply trusted that you won't face hard times alone? How does the idea of being supported—by God, others, or even your future self—change the way you approach challenges?

Dear Jesus, thank You for reminding me to remember the gift of today. I know nothing of tomorrow, but You do, and You will go before me. In Jesus's name, amen.

KINGDOM BUILDERS

For God has not given us a spirit of fear,
but of power and of love and of a sound mind.
II TIMOTHY 1:7 NKJV

How often do we waste precious energy on thoughts that don't deserve our attention? We spiral into the "what-ifs," mapping out worst-case scenarios and trying to preassemble the future like a puzzle only God can solve. And yet—how often do things actually unfold the way we feared? Rarely. Most of our imagined disasters never happen. But the toll they take? Real and exhausting. We chase control, grasp for certainty—and then God, in His grace, surprises us. The provision shows up. The door opens. The peace settles in. And what felt impossible becomes a testimony.

It's easy to believe that bold dreamers and courageous Kingdom builders operate without fear. But they don't. They've simply decided not to let fear lead. They've learned to trust the One who holds the view from the heights—even when their knees are shaking on the climb.

You are more capable than you know. Not because of your strength, but because of His Spirit. You've been called to shape eternity, not survive the moment. You can trade rehearsing what could go wrong for remembering Who goes with you. You carry the power of a sound mind—and you were made to build something eternal.

day 32

Reflect on a time when it felt like things wouldn't work out—but in the end, God brought everything together in a way you didn't expect. What did that experience teach you about trust, timing, or faith?

Dear Jesus, thank You for the reminder to focus on You and not rehearse the future based on circumstances and details I do not know. Help me trust You, taking one step at a time, believing You to provide when necessary. In Jesus's name, amen.

STOP FREAKING OUT

We demolish arguments and every pretension
that sets itself up against the knowledge of God,
and we take captive every thought to make it obedient to Christ.
II CORINTHIANS 10:5 NIV

Beth Moore once said, "You can go ahead and freak out, or you might just choose to believe that God is going to be faithful."

When panic takes over, our perspective narrows. It's like tunnel vision—we forget every answered prayer, every miracle already behind us. One unexpected curve, one unmet expectation, and suddenly we assume the worst: God must be distant. I must take control. But has He not proven Himself faithful again and again?

The moment things go "off script," we're invited to remember that our plans aren't the anchor—His presence is. Interruptions are often the very places He shows up most clearly. We don't have to fix everything or panic-protect the outcome. Instead, we can choose not to shrink in fear but to stand in faith. To raise a hallelujah, even before the outcome. To declare: He has never failed me—and He won't start now.

So, when the urge to spiral hits, pause. Breathe. Remember whom you serve. The One who sees the whole picture. The One who writes the better ending. You don't have to freak out. You get to trust a faithful God who never forgets how to show up.

day 33

Write about a time when it felt like things were out of control or you were completely on your own. Was there a moment, a shift, or something unexpected that helped you see things differently—something that reminded you of hope, support, or a greater presence at work? Reflect on what that experience taught you.

Dear Lord, thank You for being a calming Father. Help me reserve my energy for what matters, and give me the wisdom to consult You first and foremost. In Jesus's name, amen.

SHOW ME THE CHAINS

For freedom Christ has set us free;
stand firm therefore, and do not submit again
to a yoke of slavery.
GALATIANS 5:1 ESV

Even on our best days, we all carry something—something that quietly hinders us from walking fully in the freedom God offers. Some chains are loud and obvious. Others are subtle, even socially acceptable.

We all have a version of kryptonite—those habits, mindsets, or dependencies we know are draining us, but we still fear releasing. We wonder: *Who would I be without this? What if letting go costs me influence, success, or control?* So we hold tight to the very things keeping us bound. These crutches cloud our joy and chip away at our identity. But we weren't made for half-hearted living. We weren't designed for the shallow end of faith. We were created for boldness, for freedom, for deep-water trust. For lives that look different because our hope comes from a different Source.

God doesn't reveal our chains to shame us—He reveals them to free us. But freedom requires surrender. Honesty. Courage. Patience. It asks us to lay down the mask and lean into grace. Today, let's ask Him: *Show me the chains, Lord.* And let's believe that where the Spirit of the Lord is—there is not just forgiveness, but real, lasting freedom.

day 34

Ask God to show you anything that may be holding you back from fully experiencing the freedom found in Christ. Take a moment to write your prayer—and if you sense His response, feel free to write that down too.

Dear Jesus, thank You for making me free. Show me my limitations; break off my fears. Lead me in Your righteousness. In Jesus's name, amen.

DIVINELY PLACED AND PURPOSED

For if you remain silent at this time, relief and deliverance for the Jews will arise from another place, but you and your father's family will perish. And who knows but that you have come to your royal position for such a time as this?
ESTHER 4:14 NIV

Remember the boy who brought five loaves and two fish and watched Jesus feed a crowd of thousands? Or Esther, chosen as queen in a foreign land, positioned to save her people? Or Joseph, once betrayed and discarded, later elevated to power and used to preserve the lives of those who wronged him? These stories aren't fairy tales—they're faith anchors. And they carry a thread that runs through your own life: You've been divinely placed for such a time as this.

We serve a miracle-working God who delights in using the unexpected. Jesus said we would do even greater things through Him (John 14:12). That means your ordinary might be the stage for something eternal. The routine, the overlooked, the seemingly small—that's often where God plants seeds of Kingdom impact.

Today, lift your eyes. Trust His timing. And remember: He never wastes the placement of a willing heart.

day 35

Write about a time in your life when you had to wait for something you deeply desired or prayed for. How did that waiting season shape you, challenge you, or prepare you for what eventually came? Consider how God's timing was different from your own and how, in hindsight, it may have been exactly what you needed. What might God be preparing you for in your current season of waiting?

Dear Jesus, thank You for positioning me exactly where You want me to be. Make me aware of my purpose where I am and help me to do Your will. In Jesus's name, amen.

INTENTIONAL WHITE SPACE

Teach us to number our days,
that we may gain a heart of wisdom.
PSALM 90:12 NIV

How do we reach the end of the day and realize we haven't truly exhaled? We finally collapse into bed and think, *Was that a blur or real life?* We've bought into the myth that margin is for the unmotivated. But the truth? Margin is for the intentional. It's not about doing less—it's about living more awake.

White space—a quiet, unhurried moment in a busy day—invites us to come face-to-face with who we really are, not just what we've accomplished. When we stop long enough to be still without documenting it, we stop performing and start listening. To our own soul. To the Spirit of God.

Does our schedule define our worth, or does our worth shape our schedule? Do we chase fullness or wholeness? Carve out space today. Say no, trim the list, let the inbox wait. Not because you're weak—but because you're wise. In order to bring your full self into the world, you need space to meet the One who shaped that self in the first place.

You don't need a packed calendar to prove your value. You need white space to remember the Voice who named you worthy before you ever did a thing.

day 36

What does margin look like in your life right now? Where do you sense God might be inviting you to slow down, create space, or let go of something? Consider how your time, energy, and attention are being spent, and what it might mean to make room for God's presence in your daily rhythms.

Dear Jesus, remind me that white space is okay. It does not mean I am unimportant; it means I am intentional. Give me a heart of wisdom so that I may be intentional with my time and my life. In Jesus's name, amen.

WHERE FAITH AND HOPE RESIDE

And now I want each of you to extend that same intensity toward a full-bodied hope, and keep at it till the finish. Don't drag your feet. Be like those who stay the course with committed faith and then get everything promised to them.

HEBREWS 6:11–12 THE MESSAGE

Hebrews 11:1 tells us that faith is "the assurance of things hoped for, the conviction of things not seen." Faith anchors us in the present—a deep trust that God is who He says He is, even when we can't yet see the evidence. Hope, on the other hand, looks forward. It's faith with a future lens—expectant, anchored in the belief that God will be faithful in what's still to come.

But our hope often feels fragile because we place it in shaky foundations—outcomes, timelines, people, or our own plans. When hope rests anywhere but in God, it's easily stolen. Disappointment shatters it. Fear quiets it. Insecurity convinces it to back down.

When rooted in Christ, hope becomes resilient. It's not wishful thinking—it's a confident, Spirit-formed expectation that God will come through. Faith says, *The light will break through.* Hope says, *I'll keep watching for it.* And both are fueled by the deepest truth of all: we are radically, endlessly loved by a God who keeps His promises. That's where faith and hope reside—tethered to love, and held by Him.

day 37

Are there places where you've been tempted to drag your feet or give up too soon? Write about what it means to keep going with intensity, and consider how God might be encouraging you to press on—trusting that His promises are still ahead.

Dear Jesus, thank You for being the Author of my faith and the Giver of my hope. Iron out my doubts and challenge my faith so that I may be a beacon of hope to a lost world. In Jesus's name, amen.

FULLNESS OF JOY

You make known to me the path of life;
in your presence there is fullness of joy;
at your right hand are pleasures forevermore.
PSALM 16:11 ESV

Joy often feels just out of reach. We know it exists—we've seen glimpses of it in others, maybe even tasted it ourselves—but it can feel impossible to sustain. We hear the phrase "choose joy," and some days, it feels like choosing something we can't even find. But Scripture makes it clear: joy isn't manufactured; it's received. And it flows from one source—the presence of Jesus. Psalm 16:11 says, "In your presence there is fullness of joy" (ESV). Not halfway. Not sometimes. Fullness.

When we pause and sit still with Him—no performing, no perfecting—joy begins to rise. Sometimes like a gust of wind, sudden and strong. Other times, like a slow stream that seeps quietly into every corner of our soul, cleansing, softening, restoring. This joy may not look like excitement or a perfect outcome. It may not come with fireworks or laughter. But it's steady. It's healing. It whispers that we're known, loved, and held.

Joy isn't gone. It's just waiting for us to stop striving and simply be with the One who is joy. And the more we draw near to Him, the more our hearts remember: joy was never missing—it was just misplaced.

day 38

How have you experienced God's presence as a source of joy—even in uncertain or difficult times? What Scripture or truth about God sustained you during that season?

Dear Jesus, thank You for being the Light of my life and the Giver of all joy. Help me to remain in this fullness as I rest in You for the remainder of my days. In Jesus's name, amen.

ANTICIPATION VERSUS ANXIETY

Do not be anxious about anything, but in every situation,
by prayer and petition, with thanksgiving, present your requests to God.
And the peace of God, which transcends all understanding,
will guard your hearts and your minds in Christ Jesus.
PHILIPPIANS 4:6–7 NIV

We've grown used to treating uncertainty like a threat—as if not knowing demands anxiety. When the lights go out and clarity disappears, our minds race to fill in the blanks with fear. We imagine the worst, and our thoughts spiral.

But in every anxious moment, there's another path available: the road of anticipation. Anxiety assumes absence. Anticipation assumes presence. One says, *What if God doesn't?* The other says, *I can't wait to see how God will.*

When we feel out of control, we can anchor ourselves in what is certain—our God is faithful, near, and always working for our good. The darkness might surround us, but His hand is already leading us through. Right where your feet are planted is holy ground—because it's an opportunity to trust Him.

God will show up. That's settled. And whatever comes from His hand? It will be good. So take a deep breath. Choose anticipation over anxiety. The future is unknown—but it's not unheld.

day 39

What part of the future feels uncertain or makes you anxious today? In what ways could something good come from this situation? How might God use this experience to lead you toward something meaningful or unexpected?

Dear Lord, thank You for being a God of provision and for always giving me Your best. Help me choose thoughts that anticipate Your goodness instead of anxious thoughts that doubt it. In Jesus's name, amen.

INCREASED DEMAND REQUIRES STILLNESS

Yet the news about Him spread all the more, so that crowds of people came to hear Him and to be healed of their sicknesses. But Jesus often withdrew to lonely places and prayed.

LUKE 5:15–16 NIV

Jesus—the Savior of the world, the spotless Son of God—often withdrew to quiet, lonely places to pray. If He didn't live above the need for stillness and intimacy with the Father, why do we think we can?

So often, when life demands more from us, we give God less. We get the promotion or shoulder new responsibilities, and suddenly our mornings are rushed, our quiet time sidelined. We tell ourselves we'll slow down later, once things settle. But later rarely comes.

Jesus didn't wait for margin—He made it. He knew that spiritual clarity doesn't come in the chaos. It comes in the quiet. And when the pressure increased, so did His pursuit of the Father's voice.

Stillness isn't weakness—it's strategy. It's how we stay aligned, anchored, and aware. It's how we carry weight without collapsing under it. And it's not about perfect conditions. It's about choosing a quiet place—internally or externally—where God can speak and our souls can breathe.

The more that's on your plate, the more vital stillness becomes. Don't postpone what your spirit is desperate for. Step away. Breathe deep. The strength you need is found in the silence with Him.

day 40

Write down some specific times in your schedule that you can intentionally set aside to withdraw, spend time in God's Word, and be still in His presence. After you've practiced this for a day, come back and reflect—how did it go? Did you notice a shift toward greater peace or less anxiety?

Dear Jesus, thank You for being a true example of a servant. Help me to prioritize solitude with You, especially when stillness feels difficult to attain. In Jesus's name, amen.

BEING IN AWE

"Be still, and know that I am God."

PSALM 46:10 NIV

We often equate stillness with rest—as if being still means doing nothing. In a world fueled by hustle and urgency, we read "be still" as permission to collapse, catch our breath, and retreat from the noise. And in part, yes—stillness is restorative. But biblically, stillness is not passive. It's a command. A posture of surrender and reverence. It's not God saying, "Gently lay thy head." It's Him calling us to attention. A wake-up moment to stop striving, drop the illusion of control, and remember who's actually in charge.

Notice the order in Psalm 46:10: "Be still, and know." Stillness leads to knowing. It interrupts the spinning of our minds long enough to realign with the truth: God is God—and we are not.

Stillness also reframes how we respond. When anger stirs or fear rises, it gives us space to pause, to trust, to fight differently. Stillness is not inaction; it's intentionality. It's the holy pause that keeps us grounded in grace rather than reaction.

And in that still space—when our hearts bow low and our hands release—we're reminded again: God is moving. We are held. And awe is the only fitting response.

day 41

What are you fighting today? What are you striving for? What are you trying to figure out on your own? What might it look like to release the need for control and instead rest in the presence of God?

Dear Lord, thank You for who You are. As I go about my day, can You help my heart remember the importance and necessity of being still? Thank You for helping me silence my mind so that my eyes are fully opened to Your presence. In Jesus's name, amen.

LET YOURSELF BE KNOWN

Bear one another's burdens,
and so fulfill the law of Christ.
GALATIANS 6:2 NKJV

Some emotions feel easier to name than others—but loneliness? That one's tender. It catches us off guard. And no matter how old we get or how many people surround us, it still finds its way in. Even in a world full of digital connection—with texts, DMs, and constant noise—we scroll and smile and say we're fine . . . all while quietly wondering if anyone truly sees us.

And this? It breaks the heart of our Father. He sees the striving, the self-protection, the ache to be loved. And still, He stays. He whispers, *You're not alone. I've never left—not for one moment.* But He doesn't stop there. He gently invites us to take a brave step toward others—to stop patching the pain and let someone in. He reminds us that real connection isn't found in impressing, but in being honest. Not in perfection, but in presence.

We weren't created to hide behind filters or walls. We were made to be known—fully, freely, beautifully known. So drop the mask. Tell the truth. Let someone see the real you—it's God's favorite! Because love lives in the open—and that's where healing starts too.

day 42

Write about a time when you were vulnerable with a friend and it helped break down walls between you. Or think about a time when someone came alongside you and helped carry a burden. How did these experiences impact your faith or deepen your relationships?

Dear Jesus, please give me the courage to be open and the desire to be known. Thank You for removing the "lonely" label and replacing it with "loved." In Jesus's name, amen.

THOUGHTS OVERFLOW

Be careful how you think;
your life is shaped by your thoughts.
PROVERBS 4:23 GNT

The moment our feet hit the floor, our minds take off running. Before we sip our coffee, we're already thinking about that 10 a.m. meeting, how to motivate ourselves to work out, or how we'll ever tackle that pile of debt. Then come the phone notifications—each one launching a new wave of thoughts and internal noise.

It's easy to think our actions are what matter most. But Jesus reminds us that it all starts in the mind. What we dwell on shapes what we believe. And what we believe shapes everything else—including our words, our reactions, and the posture of our hearts.

Our thoughts are powerful. When we offer them to God—when we anchor them in His Word—we begin to see with clarity, hope, and peace. That's where real change begins. Not just in what we do, but in how we think and trust. A healthy, faith-filled thought life doesn't come from trying harder. It comes from soaking in truth—day by day, moment by moment.

So today, when your mind starts to swirl, pause. Ask God to speak louder than the noise. Because when His truth fills our thoughts, His peace fills our lives.

day 43

Pick a psalm and meditate on it for fifteen minutes today. Write about your experience.

Dear Jesus, thank You for giving me the power to choose my own thoughts. Help me lean into Your truth and think thoughts that bring You glory. In Jesus's name, amen.

MADE NEW

"Remember not the former things, nor consider the things of old.
Behold, I am doing a new thing; now it springs forth, do you not perceive it?
I will make a way in the wilderness and rivers in the desert."
ISAIAH 43:18–19 ESV

Maybe today's been off-the-charts good. Or maybe it's felt like a train wreck in slow motion. Or maybe—it's just getting started, and the canvas is still blank, full of quiet possibility. Wherever you are, here's the best kind of news: God is the Author of fresh starts. Tomorrow is a brand-new day—like clean-sheets-out-of-the-dryer new. And even better? You don't have to drag yesterday's bruises into it.

Scripture says His mercies are new every morning. That means you're not stuck. Not defined by the worst thing you've done or the hardest thing you've walked through. The cross declares it: You are made new. When you wake up and your body's in today but your mind is tangled in yesterday—or ten years ago—pause. Breathe. Remember who holds your story.

You've been redeemed. Restored. The past may explain part of your journey, but it does not dictate your future.

This newness? It's not shallow. It's deep enough to heal what's broken, steady what's shaken, and remind your soul that you were made to soar. Not settle. So, take that next breath. Lift your eyes. It's good to be alive—especially when Jesus is your King.

day 44

What past regrets or wounds keep replaying in your mind? What do you believe those regrets say about you—and what does God say instead?

Dear Jesus, thank You that You are always making all things new. Help me to trust You to make a way. In Jesus's name, amen.

FIRST A FOLLOWER

It is the LORD your God you must follow,
and Him you must revere. Keep His commands and obey Him;
serve Him and hold fast to Him.
DEUTERONOMY 13:4 NIV

Remember those middle school awards? "Most Likely to Lead," team captain, debate strategist? Leadership felt like the golden badge of value. Being chosen meant something: You matter. You're strong. You have influence. And leadership still holds that pull. It feels purposeful—like a sign that we're doing something that counts. But in God's Kingdom, leadership isn't about the spotlight—it's about surrender.

We can desire to lead for Jesus, and He may call us to—but if our desire to lead ever outweighs our desire to follow Him, we've missed it. Influence without intimacy is hollow. Direction without dependence is dangerous. The moment we start chasing leadership more than obedience, we risk leading others away from the very One we claim to represent.

Even Jesus—the perfect Son of God—constantly yielded to His Father's voice. His words were clear: "Not my will, but Yours." That's where true authority begins: in quiet, daily surrender.

Before we run ahead with purpose, let's pause. Let's make sure our feet are walking behind the One who leads with truth, humility, and grace. Because in the Kingdom of God, we're never called to lead without first learning how to follow.

day 45

Think about your desire to lead, influence, or make a difference—whether in big or small ways. Are there places in your life where you've tried to lead without first following God? What might it look like today to surrender that desire and trust Him to go first? Reflect on what it means for you personally to "hold fast to Him" before anything else.

Dear Jesus, thank You for being the perfect example of a leader and a follower. Help me refuse the temptation to make my name known and instead declare the greatness of who You are. In Jesus's name, amen.

BE ON THE SCENE

"Truly, truly, I say to you, whoever believes in me
will also do the works that I do;
and greater works than these will he do,
because I am going to the Father."
JOHN 14:12 ESV

Common sense tells us: If we're not present, we miss what's happening. If we skip the wedding, we miss the vows. If we're not at the table, we miss the laughter. But have we ever considered what spiritual moments we're missing—miracles, breakthroughs, glimpses of God—simply because we're not present where our feet are?

Sometimes we're so distracted—by worry, hustle, or comparison—that we walk right past what heaven is doing. God's grace covers our missed moments, but the invitation still stands: Come closer. Pay attention. Be on the scene. In some instances, the miracle on the scene is big and loud—healing, provision, breakthrough. But sometimes? It's quieter. It's the Spirit softening a bitter heart, giving clarity in chaos, or reminding you that His strength holds when yours gives out.

No one else can live your assignment. No one else can walk in your shoes. The plans God has for you aren't generic—they're hand-crafted. But they require your presence, not your perfection. So take a breath. Look up. Show up. Miracles don't always shout—they often whisper. And to witness them, we simply need to be here. On the scene.
Fully present. Fully His.

Write a prayer to God, asking Him to show you where He wants you to be present. Ask Him to shine a light on any areas of your life where you've felt distracted, distant, or hesitant to fully show up. Write down any thoughts or insights He may give you.

Dear Jesus, thank You for the plans You have crafted just for me. Will You help me to show up on the scene, ready and willing? In Jesus's name, amen.

HE IS GOD OF ALL

One God and Father of all,
who is over all and through all and in all.
EPHESIANS 4:6 NIV

How's your heart today? A little tired? Maybe stretched thin, overwhelmed, or quietly anxious beneath the surface? Before you dive into the day, take a deep breath and remember: your hope is anchored in hands that never fail. He is God of all. Not just the holy moments, but the hidden ones. The big dreams and the everyday routines. The highs that make you sing and the heartaches that bring you to your knees. He made it all. He sees it all. He carries it all—with tenderness, strength, and unshakable love.

Even the things you think are too messy, too small, or too far gone—He's already there. His presence isn't partial, and His authority isn't limited. The question isn't: *Is He in it?* The question is: *Will we invite Him to lead?* Whether we acknowledge Him or not, He is still God over this day. Over your worries. Over your weaknesses. Over the next step you don't yet see. The One who spoke galaxies into being now lives within you. You can walk in quiet confidence today—not because you have it all figured out, but because He does.

He is God of all. And that includes you.

day 47

Do you believe, without a doubt, that God is over all, even the small details in your life? Be honest. Explain your answer.

Dear Jesus, thank You for being so powerful, so mighty, and so true. When I find myself picking up the burdens or worrying about circumstances, remind me that I hope in You. In Jesus's name, amen.

BETTER BECAUSE OF THE FIRE

Their work will be shown for what it is,
because the Day will bring it to light. It will be revealed with fire,
and the fire will test the quality of each person's work.
I CORINTHIANS 3:13 NIV

Job's adult life feels like a string of relentless fires. One after another, loss scorched his world—his children, his livelihood, even his health. Grief came in waves. His body broke down. His wife urged him to curse God and walk away. But Job didn't let hopelessness have the final word. His pain was real, but so was his perspective. He wrestled—but he didn't run. In the middle of the flames, he clung to this: God is still God, even when we don't understand. God doesn't always calm the fire, but He never wastes it. And He never leaves us in it alone.

God wasn't trying to make Job's life easier. He was deepening Job's understanding of who He truly is. And when Job stopped trying to formulate explanations and started to worship, everything shifted.

Sometimes the fire doesn't burn us—it purifies us. It clarifies what's true. It reminds us that even when everything else is stripped away, the God of hope remains. Job didn't come out of the fire the same. He came out refined, restored, and rooted. And so will we. Because the fire may change us—but it cannot consume the One who holds us.

day 48

Hoping in God does not mean denying your feelings. Express your feelings to God today, like Job, while remaining hopeful in His faithfulness.

Dear God, thank You for being most concerned about the condition of my heart. Help me to seek You, to be quick to obey, and to firmly trust that You are at work. In Jesus's name, amen.

REFUSE TO BE REALISTIC; DO THE IMPOSSIBLE

Ah, Lord God! It is you who have made the heavens and the earth by your great power and by your outstretched arm! Nothing is too hard for you.
JEREMIAH 32:17 ESV

How often do we quietly limit God—not with our words, but with our expectations? We don't outright say, "Lord, You can't," but our prayers stay safe, our plans stay small, and our hearts quietly brace for disappointment. But then Jesus steps in and disrupts it all. He breathes life into the places where we've settled and whispers, *Get ready. I'm not finished. It's going to be bigger than you imagined.*

Think about it: Abraham and Sarah believed for a child long after their bodies said it was impossible. Noah built an ark before a single drop of rain had ever fallen. These weren't people with perfect faith. So what set them apart? They were people with *persistent* faith. They chose to believe God, even when it made no sense. They refused to be realistic. They trusted a God who specializes in the impossible—who multiplies what little we offer and meets us where He sends us.

Today, resist the urge to shrink your prayers to fit your comfort zone. Stretch your faith. Dare to believe again. Because the God who called you is the same God who carries you. And He's not in the business of small stories.

day 49

What dreams have you deemed unrealistic and/or illogical? Would you ever consider taking another look at the dreams you've set aside and asking God if these desires align with His will?

Dear Jesus, thank You for the ways You are calling me out of my comfort zone. Help me to focus on Your voice, forgetting what is expected or realistic. In Jesus's name, amen.

REMEMBER WHOSE YOU ARE

"Behold, I have engraved you on the palms of my hands;
your walls are continually before me."
ISAIAH 49:16 ESV

Getting lost in a grocery store as a child is terrifying. The aisles feel endless, the faces are unfamiliar, and everything just looks a little too big. But what's the first question someone asks when they see the panic in your eyes? *"Who are your parents?"* Because when you're lost, the fastest way to be found is remembering whom you belong to.

The same is true for us now. When we drift—when we chase things that never satisfy or seem to be stuck in a life that doesn't feel like ours—the way back isn't hustle or fixing ourselves. It's remembering Whose we are.

You were created on purpose. You are protected, pursued, and deeply loved by your heavenly Father. When your soul aches for comfort—when you think you're longing for routine, home, or familiar places—what you're really longing for is *Him*. He is the One your spirit is straining for. And when you whisper His name, He doesn't make you search long—He draws near.

So today, if you feel off course or unseen, pause. Lift your head. You're not forgotten. You're not too far gone. You're His. And He always comes for His own.

day 50

Describe a time when you felt lost or uncertain and turned to Jesus for comfort. What led you back to Him? How does it feel to know that Jesus is with you all the time, that He will always be the one constant you can depend on?

Dear Jesus, thank You for calling me by name and never leaving my side. When my heart forgets who I am, will You set off the alarm in my soul to return to home base? In Jesus's name, amen.

AN UNDIVIDED HEART

Draw near to God and He will draw near to you.
Cleanse your hands, you sinners;
and purify your hearts, you double-minded.
JAMES 4:8 NKJV

In a world that celebrates multitasking and nonstop connection, being fully present feels almost impossible. Even when we're physically in the room, our minds wander. We scroll while we talk. We check out while we check in. And we carry that same divided attention into our time with the Lord.

But if we want a heart anchored in hope, it can't be divided. When we compromise even a part of our trust in Him for trust in our bank account, relationships, or abilities, we're setting ourselves up for disappointment. God never asked for part of us—He invites all of us. Not because He wants control, but out of love. He knows that a split heart will always lead to a restless soul. Only an undivided heart can truly rest.

So today, pause and ask: *Where have I placed my hope? Where have I kept a backup plan, just in case God doesn't come through?* Let's give it all back to Him. Because when our hearts are fully His, peace flows. His voice becomes clearer. And we discover that the more we give Him, the more we gain. He's not asking for perfection—just our whole hearts. And He'll carry the rest.

day 51

How much of your hope is placed in Jesus? If it's less than 100 percent, whom or what else are you placing your hope in? If there's more than one, try to assign a percentage to each. What steps can you take to place your full hope in the only One truly capable of fulfilling it? Take time to reflect and explain your answer.

Dear Jesus, thank You for being dependable, gracious, and selfless. When I am tempted to place my hope in places other than You, renew my mind. In Jesus's name, amen.

WHAT DOES HOPEFUL LOOK LIKE?

But if we hope for what we do not yet have, we wait for it patiently.
ROMANS 8:25 NIV

What does it really mean to be hopeful? Is it pretending everything's fine? Constant cheerfulness despite real hardship? Or is it something deeper—something steadier?

Hope isn't blind optimism. It's choosing to believe that God is working, even when we can't yet see the evidence. Sometimes hope looks like leaping toward a dream that feels fragile. Sometimes it's whispering promises out loud when everything around you says otherwise. Hope starts in the heart, but it shows up in how we live. In our tone. Our posture. The way we talk to strangers and love our people. Hopeful hearts carry a quiet strength—a steady light that doesn't ignore the darkness but refuses to let it win.

Hopeful people aren't untouched by sorrow—they're anchored by something stronger. They know Who holds the outcome. And they choose, again and again, to believe that even here, even now, God is near and good.

That's what hopeful really looks like.

day 52

What is asking for your attention today? Is it overwhelm, discouragement, bitterness—or is it hope in all the good that is to come? How is this showing up to those around you?

Dear Jesus, thank You for giving me a hopeful heart that brings glory to Your name. When I am frustrated or impatient, remind me to prepare and pray for what is ahead. In Jesus's name, amen.

NOT JUST VALLEY VERNACULAR

"For I know the plans I have for you," declares the LORD,
"plans to prosper you and not to harm you,
plans to give you hope and a future."
JEREMIAH 29:11 NIV

Why does the word *hope* seem to echo louder when tragedy strikes or life suddenly falls apart? It's often in the valley that we cling to it most—when pain is real and answers are few. But hope was never meant to be reserved only for the hard days.

God invites us to carry hope in every moment—not just in the trenches, but on the mountaintops and through the ordinary streets of everyday life. Hope is more than a survival language. It's a posture of praise. A way of walking when the road ahead is unknown.

A hopeful heart doesn't ignore reality—it sees it clearly and still believes God is working. It paints the canvas of life with expectancy, trusting that the God who spoke the universe into being still speaks life into us today. And here's the beauty: Hope doesn't deplete with use—it deepens. Like creativity, the more we lean into it, the more it flows.

We don't draw from a shallow well. We draw from the living Word. And His river of hope? It never runs dry. So speak hope in every season. Not just when you're desperate—but because He's always worthy.

day 53

Have you ever found yourself trying to store up hope during the good times, just in case things go wrong later? Maybe you've been through a season when one hardship followed another, and now—even when life feels good—you're bracing for the next setback. What might it look like to live fully in today's hope, without fear of what's ahead, trusting that God has enough hope for both now and whatever comes next?

Dear God, thank You for giving me this wonderful life! Help me not to hoard my hope, but rather use it now, trusting You to replenish it. In Jesus's name, amen.

SO MANY UNANSWERED PRAYERS

For the LORD God is our sun and our shield.
He gives us grace and glory. The LORD will withhold
no good thing from those who do what is right.
PSALM 84:11 NLT

For as long as I can remember, my mom has begged me to keep a journal. Every time we sit down and start talking about what God is doing—what He's teaching, shifting, healing—she'll say, "Cleere, I've told you since you were sixteen: write it down. You won't remember these moments, and one day, you'll want to." And, of course . . . she was right.

I finally started. It's not fancy—some days it's just bullet points of what I'm feeling or wrestling with. But even now, just a few months in, I can see it: God really is working all things together for good. His fingerprints are all over what I once called unanswered. He hasn't been absent. He's been patient. Intentional. Faithful. Tender. Every delay had purpose. Every "no" carried kindness. And every ache I wrote down is slowly being rewritten by His grace.

God doesn't withhold good from His children. He gives better than we knew to ask for. And sometimes, keeping a record of His quiet, sustaining faithfulness helps us redefine what *good* really means. So today, if the answers feel delayed—look back. He's been there all along.
Writing a better, richer story than we imagined.

Does it feel like God is keeping something good from you? Are you willing to trust that He has your best in mind? Why or why not?

Dear God, thank You for being King of my heart and my life. As I lift my requests and prayers to You, I trust that You will respond in Your perfect power. In Jesus's name, amen.

NO TIME FOR OFFENSE

Good sense makes one slow to anger,
and it is his glory to overlook an offense.
PROVERBS 19:11 ESV

How quickly do we take offense these days? It's almost reflexive. Scroll your feed, and it's everywhere—frustration flaring, assumptions flying, tempers rising. We are a deeply offended generation, which means we've become a deeply defensive one too.

But here's the thing: Offense is a thief. It sneaks in, disguising itself as protection, but it robs us of perspective, peace, and purpose. Instead of seeing people through the lens of eternity, we shrink our world down to how it makes us feel. Our bruised pride takes the wheel, and before long, we're reacting instead of reflecting. Serving less. Loving less. Trusting less.

But the way of Jesus? It's different. He invites us to pause before we react. To remember that we are not responsible for every word spoken to us—but we are responsible for what we receive, what we carry, and what we reflect back into the world. What if we stopped wearing offense like armor and started walking in grace instead?

There's no time to waste on bitterness when you were made to radiate His heart. You are free to live unoffended—anchored in love, covered in peace, and secure in who He says you are.

day 55

In what ways are you easily offended? The next time you find yourself in a defensive posture, what steps can you take to ensure that your response reflects the heart of God?

Dear Jesus, thank You for the gift of a sound mind. Will You remind me that offense is a choice, and that even when my pride is bruised, I can count on You to rebuild me? In Jesus's name, amen.

HOPEFUL ON A TIGHTROPE

Why are you cast down, O my soul,
and why are you in turmoil within me? Hope in God;
for I shall again praise him, my salvation and my God.
PSALM 43:5 ESV

Is it really possible to be hopeful in the middle of chaos? Can we honestly believe the future is bright when today feels dim, fragile, and heavy?

Hope feels easy when life flows smoothly. But real, gritty, God-rooted hope? It's forged on the tightrope. It's on that trembling line—where one wrong move feels like it might undo everything—that we come face-to-face with the sustaining power of His presence. No one chooses the tightrope, but it's there that our feet slow and our senses sharpen. It's there that we learn the rhythm of full dependence. Jesus doesn't just cheer from below—He walks with us, whispering truth, courage, and peace as we take each shaky step forward.

Hope doesn't pretend the danger isn't real—it just believes that the One who holds us won't let us fall, even when everything else feels like it's unraveling. When solutions feel out of reach, and the ground beneath us feels unsure, remember: This is sacred ground. Not because it's easy—but because it's holy. Even here, especially here, you are held by grace. And sometimes the bravest kind of hope is simply saying, "I'm still walking."

day 56

Write about a time when you felt as if you were on a tightrope and the only thing you could do was put one foot in front of the other and place all your hope in Jesus. Do you feel as close to Jesus today as you did then? Why or why not?

Dear Jesus, thank You for the hardship, heartbreak, and hopelessness I feel in this life; they remind me that You really are my only Hope. Hold me close today. In Jesus's name, amen.

COMPARING POTHOLES

Examine yourselves, to see whether you are in the faith.
Test yourselves. Or do you not realize this about yourselves,
that Jesus Christ is in you?—unless indeed you fail to meet the test!
II CORINTHIANS 13:5 ESV

It's sneaky, isn't it? Comparison creeps in without warning. Whether it's the stage of life we're in, the way our kids behave, the depth of our spiritual disciplines, or even how much we're struggling, it's easy to start measuring our worth based on what we think we see in others.

We especially experience this when disappointment hits—our eyes drift sideways. "Why me, Lord?" we ask, glancing at someone else's lane, convinced their road looks smoother, straighter, more blessed. We start comparing potholes, forgetting that no two paths were ever meant to be identical. We assume we know the full story, but God sees the whole road. And He's not handing out cookie-cutter journeys. He's crafting a story in you that couldn't be replicated in anyone else.

The hard places? He's using them to strengthen your soul. The bumps? They're invitations to trust Him deeper. The delays? They might be protection in disguise. God's power in you is always sufficient for the exact road beneath your feet. You don't need someone else's route to fulfill your calling—you just need to walk faithfully in yours. And when you do, you'll realize: this road leads home.

Have you ever compared yourself to someone who seemed to have it all? Who was it, and what did they have that you felt you were missing? Now take a moment to list the good things God has brought into your life—blessings that are uniquely yours. Which felt better: focusing on what you don't have, or reflecting on all that God has given you? Why do you think that is?

Dear Jesus, thank You that You are a good, good Father. Remind my heart that the potholes keep me alert and redirect my hope to You. In Jesus's name, amen.

FREEDOM AT HIS FEET

Humble yourselves, therefore, under the mighty hand of God
so that at the proper time he may exalt you,
casting all your anxieties on him, because he cares for you.
I PETER 5:6–7 ESV

We go and we go and we go. We do and we do and we do. We give and we pour and we hustle, and still—we're exhausted. Our feet keep moving, but our souls are stuck in overdrive, burning out beneath the weight of invisible expectations and self-imposed standards. We carry this quiet fatigue daily. Why are we so weary? Why does peace feel elusive? And more importantly, how do we return to it?

Scripture gives us a clue. In 1 Peter 5:6–7, we're told to humble ourselves and cast every care on Him because He truly, tenderly, cares for us. That humility—laying down the need to carry what was never ours—is the doorway to freedom.

Anxiety festers when we place our trust in ourselves. But rest is born at His feet. Not when we achieve more, but when we surrender more. Not in keeping up, but in kneeling down before Him. There is a better way—one that is light, unburdened, sacred, and deeply rooted in grace. You don't have to earn your rest. You just have to receive it. He's waiting—hands open, heart steady. Come and exhale.

What have you been anxious about lately? Bring it before God today.

Thank You, Jesus, for Your willingness to take my burdens and lift my fears. When I feel my heart getting anxious, quickly remind me that You are in control. In Jesus's name, amen.

CAPTURING KEY MOMENTS

And I heard the voice of the Lord, saying,
"Whom shall I send, and who will go for us?"
Then I said, "Here am I! Send me."
ISAIAH 6:8 ESV

Key moments. Turning points. You can probably recall a few of these moments—decisions that altered the arc of your story. Maybe it was reaching out to someone sitting alone at church. Or it was turning down that job; you were unsure at the time, but now you realize God was protecting you. Sometimes these moments seem small—a quiet nudge, a quick yes, a brave no. But in hindsight, they're defining. Divine.

God uses the ordinary to birth the extraordinary. He weaves these invitations into our days—quiet chances to listen, to act, to love, to show up when it would be easier to stay distracted. While He holds the pen of our story, He invites us to participate in the plot. Through the Holy Spirit alive within us and the truth of His Word, we are equipped to notice what matters and to move when He speaks. But we only recognize these moments when our spirit slows enough to hear Him.

This is how legacy is written: one faithful step at a time, one divine moment embraced. Stay awake to the moment you're in. The whisper you obey may become the story you tell forever.

day 59

Write about a time when you heard God's voice or felt a gentle nudge pulling at your heart. Did you follow through with what He asked? What was the outcome? If you've never heard God's voice, take a moment to reflect: Have there been moments when you felt unusually drawn to do something good, offer encouragement, or take a step of faith that didn't quite make sense at the time? How did you respond, and what happened next?

Dear Jesus, thank You for every opportunity You place before me. Will You help me to be aware and willing, not letting a single key moment pass me by? In Jesus's name, amen.

THE SABBATH: NOT A SUGGESTION

By the seventh day God had finished the work He had been doing; so on the seventh day He rested from all His work.

GENESIS 2:2 NIV

The sun and stars, moon and sky. The creatures that fill the oceans, the birds that dance in trees, the animals that roam the earth. The grass beneath your feet. The rhythm of your breath, the color of your eyes, the cadence of your life. Every detail—crafted by Him. Everything good and beautiful bears His fingerprints. And still—He rested.

Genesis says, "By the seventh day God had finished His work"—finished, as in complete. Not rushed. Not half-done. Finished. Then He paused. Not because He was tired, but because He was modeling something sacred: the rhythm of rest woven into the design of creation. God's rest was not passive. It was intentional. He blessed the Sabbath, made it holy, and called it good. So, why do we treat rest like a reward instead of a command? Why do we sprint until we collapse, then wonder why we feel disconnected and depleted? If our all-powerful, never-weary God chose rest, how much more do we need it?

The Sabbath is not a side note. It's soul-repair. It's a declaration that God is in control—even when we're still. Receive it. Practice it. He's already made room for it.

day 60

What does rest look like in your life? Do you trust God enough to pause, slow down, and simply be still? Why or why not?

Dear Jesus, thank You for the gift of the Sabbath. Will You help me to see this day for what it is—a time of rest and renewal in You? In Jesus's name, amen.

THE POWER OF THE SUBCONSCIOUS

The end of all things is at hand; therefore be self-controlled and sober-minded for the sake of your prayers.

I PETER 4:7 ESV

What we meditate on matters more than we think. The things we scroll past, the conversations we rehearse, the lies we've accidentally agreed with—these all take root, especially when our guard is down. Even when we aren't consciously thinking about them, our subconscious is soaking it all in. And over time, that becomes the soil where our thoughts grow and our patterns are formed. That's why Scripture talks so often about guarding our hearts. Because what we allow to run on repeat behind the scenes will eventually shape what we believe, how we behave, and how we respond to God and others.

The subconscious is not too deep for Him to reach. His Word doesn't just meet us in the surface-level moments—it seeps into the hidden places, realigns the patterns we didn't even notice were there, and breathes fresh truth into weary hearts. So today, ask Him to renew even what you can't see. Invite Him into the places you've ignored or assumed were too tangled. He already knows—and He's already begun the work. Let your thoughts be a garden where peace, promise, holiness, and hope flourish—not just above the surface, but at the very root.

day 61

What thoughts are you storing in your subconscious mind? When your mind wanders, does it lead to thoughts of disgust or fear or regret—or does it lead to thoughts of God's never-ending love and faithfulness? Why do you think your mind is holding on to these thoughts?

Dear Jesus, thank You for the power of my mind and that I get to choose what surrounds me on a daily basis. Help me to keep watch over my ears, eyes, hands, and feet. In Jesus's name, amen.

THE FORCE OF HOPE IN WARFARE

"No weapon that is formed against you will prosper; and every tongue that accuses you in judgment you will condemn. This is the heritage of the servants of the LORD, and their vindication is from Me," declares the LORD.

ISAIAH 54:17 NASB1995

Spiritual warfare is one of those realities that's hard to wrap our minds around. We're visual people—we like to name what we're fighting. But the battle for our minds and hearts doesn't always show up in ways we can see or easily explain.

Some shy away from the topic. But pretending the fight doesn't exist only gives the enemy more room to invade. Denial invites vulnerability. If we don't stay alert and armor up, we expose ourselves—not because we're weak, but because we're unprepared. And the enemy is strategic. He loves distraction, discouragement, and distortion.

But we don't fight from fear—we fight from anchored hope. Hope is gritty, grounded confidence in Jesus, our victorious King. It's the oxygen in our lungs when the battle feels endless and the lies feel loud. Ephesians tells us to suit up: truth around our waist, righteousness on our chest, peace on our feet, salvation over our thoughts, faith as our shield, Scripture as our sword, and prayer as our power source.

And hope? It holds everything steady and keeps us walking forward.

day 62

Are you prepared for spiritual warfare? If so, how? If not, why not?

Dear Jesus, thank You for the opportunity to fight the good fight. Show me how to be victorious in every moment. In Jesus's name, amen.

HOPE FOR THE FUTURE, USED IN THE NOW

Let us hold unswervingly to the hope we profess,
for He who promised is faithful.
HEBREWS 10:23 NIV

At one of my first jobs, I started setting aside money in a retirement account. It wasn't like a normal savings fund—this one was locked until I reached a certain age. I knew it was the responsible thing to do, but truthfully, it was hard. It meant sacrificing something helpful now for the sake of something I wouldn't see for years.

That account is a small picture of how hope in Jesus works. It's for what's to come—but it also shapes how we live right here, right now. Sometimes hope feels distant. Like something stored away for heaven, but not very useful in the chaos of today. But that's not biblical hope. Hope in God is active. It anchors us when grief knocks the wind out of us, revives our weary hearts, and steadies our faith when circumstances don't make sense. His promises aren't just for "someday." They are oxygen for the soul in this very moment.

Hope doesn't deny pain; it dares to look pain in the face and say, "My God is still working. My future is still secure. And I'm still held." Because of that, you can live with courage, expectancy, and joy today.

day 63

Do you find it hard to see the final prize of eternity through your current pain and disappointment ? Why or why not?

Dear Jesus, thank You for the gift of hope. I know it is my everyday resource that allows me to fight the good fight of faith. Thank You for being my anchored foundation; You are faithful. In Jesus's name, amen.

THE HUSTLE IS SEXY

What you have learned and received and heard and seen in me—practice these things, and the God of peace will be with you.
PHILIPPIANS 4:9 ESV

How often do we find ourselves craving a different life—one that looks simpler, shinier, or more successful from the outside? We taste the idea of more—more recognition, more riches, more respect—and it's tempting. The thrill of climbing higher, collecting applause, curating a life that looks so good from a distance . . . it's seductive. The hustle is intoxicating because it masks itself as purpose.

But when the striving quiets and the spotlight dims, many realize that the gain didn't satisfy the ache. The success didn't fill the emptiness. Why? Because a life built only for self-glory will always feel hollow. Solomon, the wisest and wealthiest man of his time, had access to everything and still concluded, "Meaningless! Meaningless!" Though the hustle can be flashy, it's often a cover for a soul that's tired and trying too hard to matter.

The enemy would love for us to chase what glitters and miss what's holy. But we know better. We've seen how the race for status leaves us breathless and broken. So today, let's shift the chase. Let's run after things eternal—truth over trend, presence over performance, and Jesus over everything.

Fame fades. But faithfulness? That's the life worth living.

day 64

What are you running after that you think will be fulfilling? Is it success, approval, security, love, recognition, or something else entirely? Have you chased after similar things in the past—and if so, did they truly fulfill you? Do you sense God inviting you to slow down, surrender, or trust Him more deeply in this area? Explain.

Dear Jesus, thank You that You offer grace for every moment when I run after things that are not of You. Help me glean the wisdom I have learned, trusting in the abundant life You have for me. In Jesus's name, amen.

RECOGNIZE YOUR VILLAGE

Therefore comfort each other and
edify one another, just as you also are doing.
I THESSALONIANS 5:11 NKJV

Do you ever catch yourself longing for different friendships or wondering if you need more people around you to feel whole? It's easy to fixate on what's missing. But often, our vision blurs when our focus drifts. Sometimes we're so busy yearning for what could be that we miss the gift of what already is.

Jesus—the only perfect One—didn't collect hundreds of followers for His inner circle. He chose twelve. He walked closely with them, invested deeply in them, and didn't waste energy on who wasn't walking beside Him. Yes, He loved the crowds. But when He was with His people? It was enough.

So how are we doing with the people in our lives? Are we really seeing them? Thanking them? Loving them with our full attention?

The Father is the best connector of hearts. He doesn't make relational mistakes. The friend who shows up unannounced, the family member who checks in, the mentor who speaks truth when it's hard to hear—these are sacred assignments. You don't need a hundred people to feel known. You just need to notice the ones already standing beside you.

Gratitude turns proximity into purpose. And presence? That's how love becomes real.

day 65

When it comes to encouraging others, what feels natural to you—and what feels challenging? Think about your usual response when you see someone who could use support or affirmation. What influences the way you respond? Explain.

Dear Jesus, thank You for every person You've divinely placed in my life. Help me recognize and appreciate them for all they are to me. In Jesus's name, amen.

THE ALLURE OF GENTLENESS

Let your gentleness be evident to all.
The Lord is near.
PHILIPPIANS 4:5 NIV

When we describe God, what words come to mind? *Mighty. Sovereign. Faithful. Gracious.* We picture strength wrapped in glory; justice balanced by mercy. But how often do we consider His gentleness?

It's easy to overlook—as if it's secondary to power or truth. But in Scripture, gentleness is not weakness; it's restraint with purpose. It's the tone of a Savior who heals with a whisper and holds our hearts with hands strong enough to shape galaxies.

God's gentleness never cancels His authority. He doesn't dilute His truth to be approachable. Instead, He draws near with warmth, never in a hurry, never forceful—just deeply present. And that's what makes His touch unforgettable.

In a culture that prizes dominance and volume, gentleness cuts through the noise with a quiet kind of courage. It disarms. It dignifies. It invites. This is the posture He invites us to take—humble in tone, bold in truth, and deeply rooted in love. Let us quiet our pride and choose the strength of a soft approach. The world doesn't need louder voices. It needs hearts that echo the kindness of Christ.

Because the gentle will inherit the earth—and they just might heal it too.

day 66

How do you express gentleness in your relationships, your words, or your actions? Are there moments when it's hard to be gentle? Why do you think that is?

Dear Jesus, thank You for Your gentle nature and confident spirit. As I travel through my day, let my gentleness be evident to all. In Jesus's name, amen.

DRENCHED IN LOVE

See what great love the Father has lavished on us,
that we should be called children of God!
And that is what we are! The reason the world
does not know us is that it did not know Him.
I JOHN 3:1 NIV

We get the glowing evaluation and think, *This will make Him proud.* We catch a glimpse in the mirror—our skin radiant, our body finally reflecting our efforts—and we whisper, *Almost there.* We're publicly thanked for our service and wonder, *Did You see that, Lord? Did I earn Your affection today?* How quickly we start performing for the love that's already ours.

But the Father's love isn't based on metrics, mirrors, or merit. It's not earned in applause or physical transformation. His love is relentless—strong enough to shatter the shame we carry, tender enough to hold our hidden ache. It goes before us and outlasts us. It steadies our trembling, quiets our striving, and replaces our self-doubt with sacred belonging. His love doesn't waver based on our obedience—it anchors us in the middle of our mess. It's the kind of love that drenches, not sprinkles. It rushes past the exterior and goes straight to the heart.

You don't have to hustle to be held. You're already His. And He loves you—deeply, personally, irrevocably—right now. Let that truth wash over you today. You are loved, not because of what you've done, but because of who He is.

day 67

What voices—internal or external—make it hard to rest in the reality of God's lavish love? What might silence the voices so you can truly live each day confident in God's love?

Dear Jesus, thank You for Your crazy love for Your children. I will always come up short when trying to deserve Your love; help me accept it and embrace every drop. In Jesus's name, amen.

HOPE FOUND IN FORGIVENESS

Bear with each other and forgive one another
if any of you has a grievance against someone.
Forgive as the Lord forgave you.
COLOSSIANS 3:13 NIV

Think back to a moment when forgiveness was extended to you—when you knew, deep down, you hadn't earned it. Maybe your words wounded. Maybe your silence spoke volumes. And still, someone chose to release what they had every right to hold. That kind of forgiveness leaves a mark. Not a scar—but a sacred reminder. Because in that moment, you weren't just observing mercy. You were enveloped by it. And as healing as it is to receive that kind of love, it's even more transformative to offer it.

When we surrender our pride and give what hasn't been requested—or even deserved—we participate in something divine. Forgiveness doesn't make what happened right. It just says, "Jesus is better than my bitterness." It's not weakness. It's strength under surrender. It's walking in freedom while handing it to someone else.

And here's the beauty: Forgiveness never ends with you. It ripples—through families, through friendships, through generations. It is one of the clearest ways we reflect the heart of God. If you're holding hurt today, consider this: Hope often enters the room through the door only forgiveness can open. And Jesus stands ready to walk through it with you.

day 68

Is there someone you're holding a grievance against right now—someone who has hurt, disappointed, or frustrated you? What feelings come up when you think about that person or situation? What might one small step toward forgiveness look like?

Dear Lord, thank You for washing me as white as snow and making me blameless in Your sight. Give me the strength and grace to forgive others as You have forgiven me. In Jesus's name, amen.

BUT IT SEEMS SO SIMPLE

But I am afraid that, as the serpent deceived Eve by his craftiness, your minds will be led astray from the simplicity and purity of devotion to Christ.
II CORINTHIANS 11:3 NASB1995

Sometimes the answer feels too simple. We look for loopholes, hidden layers, or fine print. *There must be more to it*, we think. If this is really the way, why isn't everyone walking in it?

But the beauty of the gospel is in its simplicity. God is love. God is truth. He sent His Son—not to confuse or complicate, but to rescue and redeem. Jesus died in our place so we could live fully forgiven, fully known, eternally secure. That's it. The most profound truth in the universe, wrapped in mercy and sealed with grace. And yet, this simplicity isn't shallow—it's holy. It reorders our values, reshapes our hearts, and rewrites our eternity with steadfast assurance and soul-deep transformation.

So, we live in response. We love boldly. We serve generously. We forgive quickly. We shine light into dark places not because it earns us anything, but because we've already received everything.

Don't let the simplicity fool you—it's the foundation of all hope. His love is our remedy. His truth is our compass. His presence is our peace. His grace? It's more than enough. And sometimes, simple is the most sacred thing of all.

day 69

Describe how the truth of the gospel—God's love, grace, and promise of eternal life—has shaped your life. How are you currently reflecting that truth in the way you live, love, serve, and give?

Dear Jesus, thank You for being exactly who You say You are. Help my heart to be anchored in Your Word and to keep things simple in my relationship with You. In Jesus's name, amen.

SUN STANDS STILL?

So the sun stood still and the moon stayed in place until the nation of Israel had defeated its enemies.
JOSHUA 10:13 NLT

How often does fear whisper us into hesitation—right at the edge of obedience? We sense God nudging us forward, but uncertainty makes us shrink back. Scripture overflows with moments when people stepped into their fear and heaven responded.

One of the boldest? Joshua. After making a treaty with the Gibeonites, Joshua discovered five Amorite kings were joining forces against them. A daunting coalition. But God gave a clear promise: "Do not be afraid . . . for I have given you victory" (verse 8 NLT). So Joshua marched all night. No delay. And just as God said, victory was unfolding. But Joshua didn't stop there. Needing more time to secure the win, he prayed an audacious prayer: "Sun, stand still." And it did. Not because Joshua was fearless, but because his trust in God outweighed his fear. What if we lived like that? Not with recklessness, but with holy boldness?

Fear may rise. But faith rises higher. And when we dare to believe God for the impossible, we might just see the sky itself pause for His glory. Bold prayers don't intimidate God—they invite Him to do what only He can do.

day 70

Do you expect God to show up? Why or why not?
How has He shown up for you before?

Dear Jesus, thank You for how You go before me and fight on my behalf. Help me to be like Joshua, having the courage to lead the way and trusting You to make the sun stand still on my path. In Jesus's name, amen.

WORK YOUR LAND

Those who work their land will have abundant food,
but those who chase fantasies have no sense.
PROVERBS 12:11 NIV

Scripture often uses the metaphor of a farmer—planting seed, breaking hard ground, waiting in silence, and watching with hope. The soil is ordinary, but the work is holy. Growth comes slowly, not with fireworks, but with faithful, repeated obedience that trusts God with the unseen. Still, we often long for instant results. We want strength after one workout, healing after one conversation, peace after one prayer. We measure our progress by outcomes rather than obedience. But the kingdom of God doesn't work like a microwave—it moves like a seed. Quiet. Unseen. Steady. Sacred.

Proverbs says, "Those who work their land will have abundant food." Not someone else's land. Not a future version of your life. Your land—your season, your calling, your people, your pace. So tend to what's right in front of you. Don't despise the days of slow growth or hidden faithfulness. Trust that God sees every act of obedience, every seed of faith, every tilling of tired soil. A hopeful heart keeps showing up—trusting the Gardener to bring the harvest in His time.

You work the land. He works the miracle. And the ground you're standing on? It's more fertile than it feels today.

Write about a time when you achieved overnight success. Now write about a time when you put in hard work and effort on a daily basis for months or even years and finally came out on top. Which experience meant more to you? Why?

Dear Jesus, thank You for reminding me of the importance of hard work. When I find myself craving instant gratification or forming false expectations, redirect me to Your hopes for me—that I may be diligent and steadfast in all I do. In Jesus's name, amen.

FLIPPING THE SCRIPT

The tongue has the power of life and death,
and those who love it will eat its fruit.
PROVERBS 18:21 NIV

Perspective One: I'm dreading work today.

Perspective Two: I have a job—a place to show up, contribute, and grow, where God can use my presence to impact others.

Perspective One: Everyone depends on me, and I'm exhausted.

Perspective Two: I'm stretched because I'm connected to people I love and get to serve. My capacity may feel small, but His grace fills the gaps.

Perspective One: I thought I'd be married with kids by now.

Perspective Two: God hasn't forgotten me. In this season, I have margin to pour into others, grow deeply, and trust Him with the story still unfolding.

The shift is subtle, but powerful. It's not about changing the situation—it's about seeing it through heaven's lens, through the character of a God who wastes nothing and works in the unseen. When our mouths are full of gratitude, our hearts grow lighter. Praise realigns us. It silences the spiral and revives hope.

So today, instead of staying stuck in a script of discouragement, flip it. Name the gift inside the grind. Speak life into what feels lacking. Trust that God is writing something redemptive, even here.

day 72

What is your general outlook on life? Would you say you're mostly a positive person or more naturally drawn to the negative? How do you think your perspective impacts the way you live from day to day—and how does it affect the people around you?

Dear Jesus, thank You for helping me flip my perspective as I look for the ways You are moving on my behalf. I choose to speak words of life and truth today. In Jesus's name, amen.

HOPE REDEEMS WASTED TIME

These have come so that the proven genuineness of your faith—
of greater worth than gold, which perishes even though refined by fire—
may result in praise, glory and honor when Jesus Christ is revealed.
1 PETER 1:7 NIV

Regret. Even the word carries weight. And if we're honest, most of us carry some version of it. A stretch of time we'd undo if we could. A chapter marked by rebellion, confusion, striving, or silence. Maybe we wandered. Maybe we knew better. Maybe it just hurt too much to hope. And now we wonder: *Was it all a waste?*

But God. Only He can take the time we fumbled and fold it into something purposeful and beautiful. The years we'd rather forget? He repurposes them as holy ground. The parts of our story we try to skip over become places He plants deep wisdom, compassion, and resilience. Nothing is beyond His redemption and restorative power. Romans 8 reminds us that He works all things—yes, even the things we regret—for the good of those who love Him. Hope doesn't ignore the past; it transforms it. It says, "Even this can be used."

Whether you're still in that hard season, just emerging, or carrying memories from years ago—God wastes nothing. So let the ache become altar space. Let the regret become soil. Because with Him, nothing is too far gone to be made new.

day 73

Think back to a time in your life that felt "wasted." What led to that season, and what kind of pain or disappointment came from it? What did the aftermath look like? Now take a moment to reflect—can you find even one thing from that time that you're genuinely thankful for? How might God have used that season in ways you didn't expect?

Dear Jesus, thank You for being my Rock and my Redeemer. You have restored my life and covered me in grace. Give me the strength to stay on course and remind me that You make good of everything. In Jesus's name, amen.

RIGHT DOWN THE RABBIT HOLE

"You shall have no other gods before Me. You shall not make for yourself an image in the form of anything in heaven above or on the earth beneath or in the waters below."
EXODUS 20:3–4 NIV

Isn't it wild how fast our minds spiral? One moment, we're grounded—grateful, steady, moving through the day with peace. Then suddenly, a single scroll, ping, or glance sends us spinning. Maybe it's a text that tightens our chest. A headline that sinks our hope. An image that whispers lies of exclusion, insecurity, or inadequacy. A phone call that reroutes the whole day. And before we know it, we're tumbling—right down the rabbit hole of overthinking, fear, and self-doubt.

But what if, instead of picking up the phone, we turned our hearts toward the throne? The moment we step into His presence—no script needed—He's already there. Calm. Unshaken. Present. He doesn't belittle our burdens; He just knows they're not meant to be carried alone. He sees the small unravelings, the unspoken questions, and the deep-rooted fears, and He gently invites us back to the truth: We are secure. We are seen. We are His.

The rabbit hole will always be there—but so is the Rescuer. When our thoughts start racing, may we catch them, bring them captive, and place them at the feet of the One who anchors us in peace that doesn't crumble.

day 74

What is making you feel unsettled today? What is discouraging you at this very moment? What small annoyance is currently tapping you on the shoulder every other minute? Write it all out in a prayer to God below and find peace in His presence.

Dear Jesus, thank You for continually recalibrating my mind to align with Your Word. Will You keep me aware when I let the demands of this world get the best of my emotions? In Jesus's name, amen.

CONSTANT COURSE CORRECTION

Repent, then, and turn to God, so that your sins may be wiped out, that times of refreshing may come from the Lord.

ACTS 3:19 NIV

"Rerouting . . . rerouting . . ." The voice calmly echoes as we turn the wheel, realizing we've missed a turn—again. We got distracted, veered off course, and now we're too far from where we meant to be. But thankfully, the destination is still programmed in. The GPS doesn't shame us—it simply recalculates with quiet confidence and grace.

This scene plays out in our spiritual lives too. We start with sincere intentions, but detours happen. Sometimes it's distraction; other times it's due to pride, fear, comparison, or just plain exhaustion. But God doesn't revoke the journey—He reroutes us. Gently. Faithfully. Again and again, He draws us back with love. His Word is the map. His Spirit is the voice that whispers, *This is the way, walk in it*. He's not surprised when we get off track; He simply invites us to correct the situation. There's no quota on His redirection—just a continual invitation to return, re-center, and keep going. God's guidance isn't just a onetime instruction—it's a moment-by-moment mercy. Our job isn't perfection. It's surrender.

The road may bend. The winds may shift. But the destination remains secure—because our Shepherd never loses sight of us.

In what ways has your GPS—"God's Provision Service"—
let you know you were off course in the past?
On your path today, are you open to being rerouted,
or are you determined to stay the course no matter what?

Dear Jesus, thank You for never failing to help me get back on track, no matter how far I have strayed. When I fear the consequences, remind my heart that repentance is the only way to hope. In Jesus's name, amen.

LASTING SELF-CARE

For you formed my inward parts;
you knitted me together in my mother's womb.
I praise you, for I am fearfully and wonderfully made.
Wonderful are your works; my soul knows it very well.
PSALM 139:13–14 ESV

Self-care is everywhere. Smoothie bowls, long walks, deep breaths, slow mornings—our world is saturated with strategies to help us feel better, calmer, healthier. And while none of these are bad, many fall short of what our soul is really asking for. Because self-care without soul-care only soothes symptoms. It might quiet the ache for a moment, but it won't heal what's buried deeper. Without tending to the roots, we'll spend our lives rearranging surface things—comfortable but still craving.

Lasting self-care, on the other hand, starts with surrender. It looks like nourishing your body and renewing your mind. Moving your body in strength and resting in God's presence. Making space to enjoy beauty and pausing long enough to thank the One who created it. Our goal isn't just a calmer life, but a centered soul. Not just wellness, but worship.

We were made in His image. And every act of true self-care—when rooted in truth—is really a return to that image. We don't just need a better routine. We need a deeper rhythm. And the kindest thing we can do for ourselves is to stay close to the One who made us whole.

day 76

Reflect on the difference between self-care and soul-care. How can taking care of your body also help you grow spiritually? How might you bring more gratitude, greater peace, and a sense of purpose into your self-care routines?

Dear Jesus, thank You for giving me the body, mind, soul, spirit, and heart that You did. Remove my selfishness and set my eyes on You. In Jesus's name, amen.

HOPE OF IMPERFECT PROGRESS

Not that I have already obtained all this,
or have already arrived at my goal,
but I press on to take hold of that
for which Christ Jesus took hold of me.
PHILIPPIANS 3:12 NIV

Think of something you're good at now—maybe cooking, decorating, playing an instrument, or leading a team. It probably didn't start out that way. Even natural talents require practice and intentional repetition.

Progress takes showing up consistently despite the misses, the fear of failing, and the doubt that whispers you'll never get there. And that's where hope lives—in the small, unseen, faithful steps. It's not flashy or fast. But it's forming something holy. Every time you try again, you're becoming stronger. More rooted in who God says you are. You're proving that your identity isn't found in perfection, but in perseverance with Jesus.

The world chases polished outcomes, but God honors faithful obedience. He's not tracking your missteps; He's celebrating your progress. Success isn't built on occasional inspiration, but on consistent surrender.

So, how are you showing up? With honesty? With hope? With a willingness to be shaped, even when it feels slow? God isn't asking you to be flawless—just faithful. And when your heart stays rooted in Him, even your stumbles can be sacred.

day 77

Take a moment to reflect on your journey right now. What does it look like for you to take one step at a time, even when the road ahead feels long or uncertain? In which areas of your life do you feel God inviting you to persist, stay consistent, and trust Him with the small, everyday progress?

Dear Jesus, thank You for being a God who never expects perfection but simply asks me to surrender my all. Help me to be okay with growing slowly or differently than expected, because I know that my hope is in You. In Jesus's name, amen.

REDEEMING OUR ROOTS

Rooted and built up in him and established in the faith,
just as you were taught, abounding in thanksgiving.
COLOSSIANS 2:7 ESV

Have you ever watched how bamboo grows? It's fast. Persistent. All it needs is water, and it stretches upward, cell by cell. But it doesn't grow alone—bamboo is a colony plant. It multiplies by drawing energy from its community and expanding its root system. It spreads through sidewalks, scales fences, and even breaks through concrete foundations if left unchecked. To truly eliminate bamboo, you can't just cut it back. You have to deal with the root.

Self-rejection is the same way. We think we can manage it on the surface—mask it with performance, numb it with distraction, hide it under praise. But until we let God dig up what's buried beneath—the lies, the shame, the distorted narratives—it keeps coming back, quietly overtaking what He's trying to grow.

The beauty of our Redeemer? No root is too deep, tangled, or hidden for Him to reach. He restores what we believed was broken beyond repair. He plants truth where pain once grew. The same God who paints sunsets and calls oceans to the shore calls you His masterpiece. So let Him tend to the soil of your soul—He's not afraid of your roots. He's ready to redeem them.

day 78

What roots need to be removed in your life?
Ask God to start the process of removing them.

Dear Jesus, thank You for establishing my worth long before I came to be. Will You help me find the roots that must be removed and give me the courage to do so? In Jesus's name, amen.

"WHO DO YOU SAY THAT I AM?"

"In the same way, let your light shine before others,
that they may see your good deeds
and glorify your Father in heaven."
MATTHEW 5:16 NIV

Imagine Jesus looking you in the eyes and gently asking, "Who do you say that I am?" The same question He asked His disciples, now asked of us. We'd probably answer quickly, "You're Lord!" "You're the great I Am!" Our mouths might speak what we've been taught, what we know in our heads to be true.

But if someone watched our lives on silent—no captions, no commentary—what would they say we believe about Him? Do we say He's Provider, yet live as if everything depends on us? Do we call Him Peace, yet let anxiety narrate our days? Do we proclaim Him Lord, while giving our best energy to everything but Him? The way we *really* answer this question touches every corner of our lives. It shapes how we respond to pressure, how we love people, and how we carry both pain and joy.

Jesus doesn't ask this to test our theology; He asks it to draw us closer to Him. To remind us of who He's always been. To help our hearts trust Him more deeply. So today, may our lives whisper back with love and conviction: *You're mine, Jesus. My center. My strength. My steady place to land.*

day 79

If your life was a movie without sound, how would it answer Jesus's question, "Who do you say that I am?" In what ways does your life show that you believe? In what ways does you life show your disbelief?

Dear Jesus, thank You that You are exactly who You say You are at all times. Help me to be firm in my following so that others know I trust only in You. In Jesus's name, amen.

A WORLD OF IMAGE BEARERS

And to put on the new self,
created after the likeness of God
in true righteousness and holiness.
EPHESIANS 4:24 ESV

What if we spent less time perfecting our own image and more time pointing out the image of God in others? How would the world shift if we were less self-conscious and more God-conscious—especially in the way we see one another?

Instead of competing, we'd find connection. Instead of comparison, we'd discover community and compassion. We'd see the fingerprints of our Creator in every face, every laugh, every story—not something to critique, but something to celebrate. When we fix our eyes on how others reflect His beauty, our own insecurities begin to loosen their grip. The pressure to perform fades, and delight grows in its place. Peace settles in, and love multiplies.

And most importantly, we'd keep returning to the One who formed us. When questions rise about how we were made or why we feel like we are too much or not enough, we'd let Jesus speak into it. His voice is healing. His love is steady. His Word is our mirror. And as we'd soak in His presence, we'd learn to see what He's always seen—image bearers, through and through. He called it very good. Let's live like we believe Him.

How often do you take time to recognize God's image in others? Do you find joy in the unique differences of those around you, knowing that God intentionally created each of us distinctly? If you do, how has this perspective shaped the way you interact with others? If not, what do you typically look for in people, and how might shifting your focus change your relationships?

Dear Jesus, thank You for creating me in Your image. Help me to be diligent in looking for Your beauty within myself and those around me. In Jesus's name, amen.

A GOD OF SYSTEMS

"This is what the Sovereign Lord says: Look! I am going to put breath into you and make you live again!"
EZEKIEL 37:5 NLT

The circulatory system. The digestive system. The solar system. The water cycle. From the galaxies above to the organs within, we live surrounded by—and sustained through—systems. From the beginning of time, God has been a God of order, rhythm, and intentional design. He orchestrated the human body with twelve intricate systems that function in harmony, each depending on the others to help us move, breathe, think, and live. He designed ecosystems that respond to change and restore balance. His fingerprints are everywhere, revealing a deep love for structure that sustains life.

If God embedded systems into the universe, wouldn't He also care about the patterns and rhythms shaping our everyday lives? The way we steward our time, the habits we build, and the pace we choose all impact our capacity to receive from Him and respond to Him.

Systems are not about perfection, but alignment. They're meant for sustainability, not control. So today, let's pay attention to the rhythms we carry. Let's build systems that make space for peace, for purpose, and for the presence of the One who holds it all together.

day 81

How does your daily routine shape your thoughts and habits? Are there any areas where chaos or disorganization might be clouding your ability to hear from God? If so, ask Him to show you how to move in better rhythm with His grace.

Dear Jesus, thank You for being a God of order, of freedom, and of grace. Remind me that efficiency is not separate from rest or joy. In Jesus's name, amen.

THE WALK TO THE CROSS

Then He said to them all:
"Whoever wants to be My disciple must deny themselves
and take up their cross daily and follow Me."
LUKE 9:23 NIV

"Lord, where are You? What am I supposed to do with this?" We whisper questions into the ache, unsure of what's ahead. We keep moving—barely—but then we see the cross. Distant at first, but familiar. As our eyes adjust and the dust of discouragement settles, we feel the weight shift. Not because the burdens disappeared, but because we're not carrying them alone anymore. We set our bags down. We lift our heads. And there He is—arms stretched wide, love poured out. "Oh," we remember, "You've already done it all for us."

Hope isn't a fleeting feeling—it's what fuels our footsteps when strength has run dry. It's what anchors us when surrender feels like loss but is really the beginning of victory. It's what lets us grieve and believe, wrestle, and then trust.

The walk to the cross isn't just a onetime journey. It's daily. Relentless. Holy. Sometimes it's quiet and lonely, and other times, it's filled with worship and tears. When your legs feel too tired to keep going, don't power through alone—ask Him to carry you. The road may be hard, but the destination is always love. Always life. Always redemption. Always hope.

day 82

Describe a recent struggle. At what point did you realize that your white flag was the marker of your victory, and not your defeat?

Dear Jesus, thank You for reminding my soul that I must take up my cross daily. You are my hope. In Jesus's name, amen.

SUSTAINING ABUNDANCE

And God is able to bless you abundantly,
so that in all things at all times,
having all that you need,
you will abound in every good work.
II CORINTHIANS 9:8 NIV

What comes to mind when we think of abundance? Likely a picture of overflow—jars spilling over, pantries stocked full, lives filled to the brim. But biblical abundance goes deeper than supply; it touches the soul and redefines provision. When Scripture speaks of God's abundance, it's never just for hoarding—it's always for pouring.

God fills us with more than enough—not so we can build bigger barns, but so we can build deeper relationships. So we can forgive generously, listen attentively, and show up sacrificially. The kind of abundance that sustains is rooted in surrender, not striving. We sustain it not by grasping tighter, but by trusting deeper. We remember: the well we draw from is not dependent on our hustle, but on His heart and eternal faithfulness.

True abundance isn't found in what we earn, accumulate, or even deserve—it's found in the unshakable Source of it all. And when our souls know where the fountain is, we stop striving for the overflow . . . and start living from it.

day 83

Write about what "giving" means to you. Does it feel like an act of worship, a routine, a burden—or something else entirely? Has God ever led you in this area?

Dear Jesus, thank You for being a God of abundance and for giving me a full life. Will You help me to have open hands and a generous heart, remembering that the greatest riches are those I give away? In Jesus's name, amen.

IDENTITY-DRIVEN PURPOSE

For we are God's handiwork,
created in Christ Jesus to do good works,
which God prepared in advance for us to do.
EPHESIANS 2:10 NIV

It's the quiet ache beneath so many of our questions: Am I living a life of purpose? We long to know that when we wake up, place our feet on the floor, and move through our day, it matters. That we're building something eternal—not just surviving the hours.

God delights in our desire to do good works and move His kingdom forward. But sometimes, in our pursuit of purpose, we unknowingly slip into striving. We measure meaning by output and let our doing define our being. Slowly, purpose becomes the driver of our identity, and the weight of productivity overshadows the joy of simply being God's child.

But identity was always meant to come first. When we walk in the truth that we are deeply loved, chosen, and called, we become unshakable before even lifting a finger. No role, title, accolade, or missed opportunity can alter the value God has placed on us.

You are not wasting your life when you walk with Him. Even the unseen steps, ordinary days, and quiet obedience are steeped in meaning. Purpose will naturally flow from a life rooted in identity. And in that place, peace and direction find you. Every single time.

day 84

What does a "significant life" mean to you? What qualities or experiences do you believe define a life well-lived? Are you focused on finding your purpose in life? Or are you focused on serving Jesus? Do you see those two pursuits as separate, or deeply connected? Explain.

Dear Jesus, thank You for establishing my identity firmly in You. As I approach my day and my schedule, let me follow as You lead. In Jesus's name, amen.

WHO HAS THE MICROPHONE?

Let the word of Christ dwell in you richly in all wisdom, teaching and admonishing one another in psalms and hymns and spiritual songs, singing with grace in your hearts to the Lord.
COLOSSIANS 3:16 NKJV

From the moment we were formed in the womb, voices have shaped us—those of our parents, teachers, peers, culture. As children, we absorbed whatever was said about us, often without filter or question. But as we grow, a sacred responsibility emerges: we get to choose who holds the microphone.

Whom are we allowing to speak into our soul? Who gets the final word on our identity?

Far too often, we hand the mic to voices that are loud but not wise—critics from the cheap seats of our lives. We let old wounds, human opinions, or social expectations narrate our worth. We assume that those who love us are always right. But love without truth can still wound.

When Jesus holds the microphone, everything changes. His voice is steady and sure. He speaks not to tear down, but to build up, calling out who we really are—not just who we've been. His words silence shame, strengthen weary hearts, and anchor us in peace.

You have the authority to reclaim your narrative. Hand the microphone to the One who knows you fully and loves you still. Let His truth be the loudest voice you hear today—and let it rewrite every lie.

day 85

Whom are you listening to and why?

Dear Jesus, thank You for the gift of Your affirmation and truth that You pour into me. Help me chase Your will, not the agreement of those around me. In Jesus's name, amen.

A TEACHABLE SPIRIT

Hold on to instruction, do not let it go;
guard it well, for it is your life.
PROVERBS 4:13 NIV

We are forever students in this thing called life. We're learning how to navigate new seasons, walk through patches of disappointment, steward the relationships we've been entrusted with, and become people who reflect the heart of Jesus. And when it comes to the school of life, honor roll is measured a little differently than we might expect.

A teachable spirit knows its posture. We stand as sons and daughters of the Most High King—anchored in grace, shaped by truth, and positioned to grow. It means we listen to His voice, especially when it lovingly interrupts our assumptions or redirects our plans. We resist the urge to act like we know everything and instead lean into the One who truly does.

Spiritual maturity doesn't come from having all the answers; it flows from being willing to keep asking the right questions. It's found in the humility to pause, the courage to admit we don't know, and the faith to follow His leading even when it feels unfamiliar or risky.

May we stay softhearted, openhanded, and always willing to learn. The world doesn't need perfect people—it needs humble ones, rooted in wisdom and led by love.

day 86

Would you describe yourself as having a teachable spirit? Why or why not?

Dear Jesus, thank You for giving me a teachable spirit. Humble me when I want to become the teacher, and make Your authority known to me in every moment. In Jesus's name, amen.

MARGIN MULTIPLIES

He has shown you, O man, what is good;
and what does the LORD require of you but to do justly,
to love mercy, and to walk humbly with your God?
MICAH 6:8 NKJV

Isn't it wild how nearly any task or role will expand to fill every inch of time we give it? Work doesn't shrink to fit within our boundaries—it stretches to occupy every open space. That's why margin never happens by accident. It must be chosen—guarded, even.

When we carve out time to be still, something sacred happens: Our soul remembers who it is. We find ourselves more open to wonder and drawn to small joys again—a slow walk around the block, an old book cracked open at a coffee shop, hands back in the soil. We begin to hear God in places we'd forgotten to listen.

Margin isn't wasted time. It's holy ground where rest revives, creativity flows, and purpose gets refocused. It multiplies far more than just time; it multiplies clarity, joy, and the awareness of God's presence. When we make room, we become more compassionate friends, more grounded leaders, more patient parents, and more fully alive people. Not because we hustled harder—but because we allowed space for God to speak into the noise.

The invitation is simple: make margin. Let God fill the quiet. And watch how your life, your peace, and your purpose multiply.

day 87

When was the last time you enjoyed free time? What did you do? How do you think this time impacted you personally, and those around you?

Dear Jesus, thank You for creating the gift of time and for guiding me in how to spend that time. Show me how to create margin in life, and teach me how to be still with You. In Jesus's name, amen.

ACTION OVER INTENTION

For the word of God is living and active and sharper than any two-edged sword, and piercing as far as the division of soul and spirit, of both joints and marrow, and able to judge the thoughts and intentions of the heart.
HEBREWS 4:12 NASB1995

When it comes to intentions, it's probably fair to say that most of us live our lives meaning well. We want to prioritize health, love our people well, chase our callings, and live intentionally. Our hearts are full of hope, and our minds full of lists. But if we're honest? Intention alone hasn't carried us very far. We can look back and trace the gap between what we hoped for and what actually happened. Dreams unpursued. Promises unkept. Good ideas left behind. Why? Because intention is easy—action costs something. It requires margin, discipline, and the courage to follow through.

Even in our walks with God, desire isn't enough. We can long to be near Him, hear His voice, and feel His peace—but until we show up and make space, we'll miss the depth we were made for. He doesn't expect perfection, just presence. He meets us in the effort—in the showing up, the quiet prayers, the hard "yes." When we choose action over just hoping for it, we begin to see real growth.

Let's be people who don't just mean well. Let's move. Start small, stay faithful, and trust that He'll meet you in every step.

day 88

In which areas is God inviting you to move from intention to action—especially when it comes to spending still, focused time with Him? What is one small, consistent change you can make this week to start living out what you say matters most?

Dear Jesus, thank You for giving me a proactive spirit and an attitude of excellence. Help me line up what I do with what I say and who You are. In Jesus's name, amen.

THE HOPE OF JOSEPH

As for you, you meant evil against me,
but God meant it for good in order
to bring about this present result,
to preserve many people alive.
GENESIS 50:20 NASB1995

When we read Joseph's story in Scripture, it's easy to focus on the outcome and forget the agony that came before. But Joseph was human—just like us. Betrayed by his brothers. Sold into slavery. Wrongfully imprisoned. Forgotten. His story wasn't just hard—it was heartbreaking. And yet, again and again, Scripture reminds us: "The LORD was with Joseph" (Genesis 39:2, 21, 23 NASB1995). In the pit. In the prison. In the waiting. God's favor didn't always look like deliverance—it looked like presence. And that presence sustained him in both suffering and silence.

As a boy, Joseph had bold dreams of leadership. But the path to those dreams looked nothing like what he'd imagined. From the outside, his life may have looked like a series of setbacks. But heaven saw preparation. Every betrayal and delay shaped him for the palace.

We serve a God who redeems what feels wasted. Who writes redemption into every chapter of our lives. Just as He was with Joseph, He is with you—in the waiting, the confusion, the holding pattern that makes no sense . . . yet. He is forming something far bigger than you can see. So hold on. Where His presence is, hope is not just possible—it's unstoppable.

day 89

Write about a current situation you're facing—whether it feels challenging, uncertain, or simply ordinary. Then imagine and describe the best possible outcome, even if it feels far off or unlikely. *(Remember: Joseph's journey took him from slavery to becoming the second-most-powerful man in Egypt.)* God specializes in using unlikely paths to fulfill extraordinary purposes. So dream boldly. What might God be shaping in you through today's circumstances?

Dear Jesus, thank You for Your ability to use any and every situation for my good and Your glory. Open my eyes like You did for Joseph, so that I may see the workings of Your hands even in the hardest places. In Jesus's name, amen.

GET SILENT; LISTEN UP

"My sheep hear my voice, and I know them, and they follow me. I give them eternal life, and they will never perish, and no one will snatch them out of my hand."

JOHN 10:27–28 ESV

Have you ever noticed that the words *silent* and *listen* are made up of the exact same letters? It's not just a clever coincidence—one can't happen without the other. To truly listen for God's voice, we must first become still. And stillness doesn't just mean quiet surroundings—it means a quiet soul anchored in trust.

Sometimes the loudest voices in our lives aren't external—they're the anxious thoughts running wild in our minds. We move from one thing to the next, begging God for direction, all while never stopping long enough to actually hear His whisper in the waiting. But when we slow down? When we make space for silence and lean in close? His voice becomes familiar. Personal. Steadying. We are His sheep—His beloved—and He delights in leading us gently, not forcefully, into wide-open spaces of peace and purpose.

In His presence, there is no pressure to perform—just a place to belong and be known. And the more time we spend with Him, the more we begin to carry His hope into every corner of our lives.

He's always speaking. We just need to get quiet enough to hear.

day 90

Spend fifteen minutes in total stillness and silence and *just be* with the Lord. Write about your experience.

Dear Jesus, thank You for reminding me of the importance of getting still and silent so that I may listen well. Help me to have the confidence of hearing Your voice, and give me the courage to follow through with Your instructions. In Jesus's name, amen.

IN OVER OUR HEADS

"I have said these things to you, that in me you may have peace.
In the world you will have tribulation. But take heart;
I have overcome the world."
JOHN 16:33 ESV

Is it wise to keep going when everything around us screams, "You won't make it"? Logic tells us to turn around. Culture tells us to play it safe. But faith invites us into deeper waters.

No one escapes the ache of life untouched. Loved ones leave sooner than our hearts can handle. Marriages fracture under secrets no one saw coming. Diagnoses rearrange dreams that were within our grasp. Bank accounts dry up while bills keep arriving. And just when we feel steady again, another wave knocks us down. Life's unpredictable, and some days we're simply in over our heads.

But here's the hope: What's over our head is always under Jesus's feet. He doesn't just meet us in the storm—He stands above it, inviting us to cast our burdens onto His shoulders. Not because we're weak, but because we were never meant to carry them alone.

Freedom isn't found in figuring it all out. It's found in surrender—placing everything that feels too heavy at the feet of the One who holds authority over it all. When we let go, we're not giving up. We're giving it to the only One who can redeem it. And He always does.

day 91

What burdens do you need to lay at Jesus's feet right now? How would it feel to be able to leave these at the feet of God and simply walk away?

Dear Jesus, help me stay at Your feet; I trust You with everything. Warm my heart as I remember that You never let me go. In Jesus's name, amen.

TAKE A BREAK

"Come to me, all who labor and are heavy laden,
and I will give you rest. Take my yoke upon you, and
learn from me, for I am gentle and lowly in heart,
and you will find rest for your souls.
For my yoke is easy, and my burden is light."
MATTHEW 11:28–30 ESV

What comes to mind when you think about Sabbath rest? For many of us, it's uncomfortable. Rest feels unproductive, almost irresponsible. The world keeps spinning, our to-do lists don't shrink, and perfectionism whispers that stillness is laziness. So we push, strive, and hustle—hoping it earns us peace that never quite settles in. But Sabbath rest isn't about pausing because the work is done—it's about trusting that God is the One who finishes what He starts and sustains what we can't.

Sabbath is a sacred rhythm, a weekly exhale woven into our design. It's where our bodies recharge, our minds quiet down, and our souls return home. In Sabbath, we're reminded that our value isn't tied to our output, but to our identity as deeply loved children of God.

The world might applaud constant motion, but heaven blesses the one who knows when to stop. Sabbath delights the heart of our Father—not because we're producing, but because we're present. In the quiet, we're reminded that we are more than what we do. We are free to simply be.

So, take the break. Your soul needs it. And God delights in it.

day 92

When we give our first to Jesus, offering this time to Him and to ourselves, He replenishes our time and provides all that we need to walk out His will. What would you gain from a weekly day of rest? What would you lose?

Dear Jesus, help me to relinquish the noise and activity to take time to rest. I delight in this time with You as I let Your love wash over me. In Jesus's name, amen.

SPEAK THE TRUTH TO YOURSELF

Let the words of my mouth and the meditation of my heart be acceptable in your sight, O Lord, my rock and my redeemer.

PSALM 19:14 ESV

You know your words can build up or break down others—but do you realize how much they shape you?

Your soul is always listening. The way you speak—especially to yourself—becomes the atmosphere you live in. When your words are laced with fear, comparison, or defeat, your body carries it: shoulders heavy, joy distant, courage dim. But when your lips echo truth—when you remind yourself of God's goodness, nearness, and promises—you begin to walk lighter, think clearer, and hope deeper.

If every word you spoke became your reality, what kind of life would you be building? Would you be paving the road toward peace and purpose, or reinforcing the path of fear and self-doubt? Your tongue holds the power of life and death (Proverbs 18:21). And that includes the life you're cultivating within.

You are not at the mercy of your emotions or circumstances. You are anchored by truth—and it's your job to speak it. Preach the gospel to your own heart. Call out what's holy. Prophesy joy. Declare freedom. Say what is true—even when it feels shaky. Because the more you speak it, the more your soul will believe it.

day 93

In which areas of your life do you need to separate facts from feelings? Write down what *feels* true and contrast it with what you actually know to *be* true.

Dear Jesus, let me choose to rejoice and to see things through Your eyes. Help me to feel what I'm feeling without making a home there; help me to speak the truth to myself. In Jesus's name, amen.

LOST, BUT NOT HOPELESSLY LOST

If we confess our sins, he is faithful and just to forgive us our sins and to cleanse us from all unrighteousness.
1 JOHN 1:9 ESV

Have you ever looked up and realized you've wandered far from where you meant to be—spiritually, emotionally, or even physically—and thought, *How will I ever get back?*

Sometimes, what feels like hopelessness is actually just misdirection. We sense the dissonance between our heads and our hearts—our minds know we've drifted, but our feet keep walking. Guilt whispers, *It's too late.* Shame says, *You should've known better.* And suddenly, we believe the lie that our sin—our detour—has disqualified us.

But here's the truth: Repentance isn't about punishment—it's about pivoting. It means turning around and returning to the One who always knows the way home. Jesus doesn't meet us at the finish line once we've fixed ourselves—He meets us on the road, offering direction, grace, and a fresh start. He's the Good Shepherd who leaves the ninety-nine to pursue the one who strayed away. The Way-Maker in your wilderness. The Light when the path feels dim.

You may feel lost, but you are never beyond His reach. When He leads, even the long way around becomes a road to redemption.
Hope is not gone—it's just waiting for you to turn back.

day 94

What is holding you back from an authentic relationship with Jesus? What is in the way—what are those things you hide, push down, or pretend don't exist just so you can move forward without confronting them? Write a prayer to Jesus today and lay these things at His feet.

Dear Jesus, You have never left me. Help me remember that my best is still ahead when I trust in You. In Jesus's name, amen.

A MASTERPIECE OF GOD'S MAKING

I praise You because I am fearfully and wonderfully made;
Your works are wonderful, I know that full well.
PSALM 139:14 NIV

When you look in the mirror, do you see a masterpiece? If you're like most of us, you probably see the cracks. The regrets. The scars and unfinished pieces you wish looked different. But that's not what God sees. He sees His child—redeemed, radiant, covered in Christ. Where we see imperfection, He sees intentionality.

Learning to see ourselves through His eyes is a practice. When we start the day, we can speak life over who we are and Whose we are. We can thank Him for breath in our lungs and grace that covers what we can't yet see clearly. As we move through our day, we get to choose how we view others too—not through comparison or criticism, but with eyes tuned to beauty. The more we train our hearts to recognize God's fingerprints on those around us, the more we'll notice His handiwork in ourselves. Like standing before a painting and realizing the detail you once overlooked, we begin to value what we once dismissed.

You are not a project. You are not a problem to solve. You are a masterpiece of God's making—beloved, becoming, and already deeply beautiful in His eyes.

What do you see when you look at yourself? What does God see? Explain the differences in these answers.

Dear Jesus, I am Your masterpiece, fearfully and wonderfully made. Help me to absorb that truth so it radiates through my entire being and changes the way I see everything. In Jesus's name, amen.

VOICES IN OUR HEADS

The wise in heart accept commands,
but a chattering fool comes to ruin.
PROVERBS 10:8 NIV

When God tells us who we are, do we believe Him?

Too often, His voice sounds like a whisper while the world shouts in our ears. The court of public opinion grows loud, and instead of handing God the mic, we pass it around, desperate for affirmation, chasing approval, and tuning our identity to the volume of others. We may hear some truth, but we let others' opinions carry equal weight with God's Word. We absorb their praise or criticism as gospel, forgetting that only One knows the depths of our soul and the dreams He knit into our bones.

God invites us to seek wise counsel, but when those voices clash with His truth, He gently asks us to hand the mic back to Him. What has He declared about you? What truth has He already spoken?

We must choose who holds the loudspeaker over our lives. And just as importantly, we must steward the responsibility of the words we speak over others. May our voices echo heaven, not opinion. And may we always be a people who turn down the noise and lean into the One who speaks identity, value, and destiny with perfect love.

day 96

Who speaks the loudest in your life? Do you think they fully understand the influence they have on you? Do you recognize the weight of that influence? Explain.

Dear Jesus, I ask that You give and take away the loudspeaker from whomever You see fit in my life. Help me to listen to You above all others. In Jesus's name, amen.

MAKING SPACE

Yet the news about Him spread all the more, so that crowds of people came to hear Him and to be healed of their sicknesses. But Jesus often withdrew to lonely places and prayed.

LUKE 5:15–16 NIV

Give more, get more—right? That's the rhythm we often fall into. We overextend ourselves, thinking the extra effort will finally earn us the breakthrough, the promotion, the affirmation we crave. Even in our closest relationships, we operate like investment bankers—expecting a return on every ounce of energy we pour out. But what if the real return comes not from giving more, but from making space?

Our minds fill quickly—with goals unmet, people to care for, and standards that seem just out of reach. If we're not careful, life becomes a blur of obligation, and stillness becomes something we have to fight for instead of something we regularly protect.

Margin doesn't magically appear. It must be chosen, carved out, and fiercely honored. Creating space in our schedule isn't weakness—it's wisdom. It's how we stay healthy enough to show up with clarity, strength, and joy.

Contrary to what our culture says, stillness isn't a waste of time—it's where we're most likely to meet with God. When we slow down, we remember who's actually in charge. And in that sacred space, we realign our hearts with what matters most. That's not loss. That's life.

day 97

In what ways does "scheduling margin" work for you? Maybe blocking off time on your calendar, building in space between commitments, making sure to have one evening a week when you don't make plans?

Dear Jesus, thank You for multiplying the time I give You and guiding me down a path of diligence. Help me to make space instead of consuming every inch of space I have. In Jesus's name, amen.

GET OFF THE RIDE

Hope does not disappoint, because the love of God has been poured out within our hearts through the Holy Spirit who was given to us.

ROMANS 5:5 NASB1995

Do you ever feel like you're strapped into a roller coaster—soaring with joy one moment, spiraling with fear the next? It's exhausting. The dips come without warning. The twists disorient us. We ride the highs of good news and the lows of worry, clinging to the illusion of control while life rushes past in a blur.

But hope—real, soul-steadying hope—isn't found in smoother tracks or predictable turns. It's found in the unchanging character of God. He is always present. Always sovereign. Always faithful. A hopeful heart is not one that avoids pain or denies reality; it's a heart anchored to truth in the middle of uncertainty. It says, "Even here, I trust You."

We weren't meant to live reactive lives, tossed by every wave of emotion or circumstance. We were meant to live anchored—feet steady, heart fixed, eyes set on Jesus.

Let's be people of holy expectation, who remain rooted when life shakes, who hope even when the headlines don't, who reflect the calm of Christ in a chaotic world.

Get off the ride. Lay your fear down. And let your faith do the standing when everything else wants to pull you under.

day 98

What does it mean to have hope in Jesus? What does it mean to be loved by God? Write about a time when you held on to this hope and this love when bad news hit.

Dear Jesus, give me the courage to have a heart that is hopeful in You, no matter what tomorrow brings. Thank You for the mercies You provide that are new each morning. In Jesus's name, amen.

THE SOLUTION TO NO SOLUTIONS

Trust in the LORD with all your heart,
and do not lean on your own understanding.
PROVERBS 3:5 ESV

Think back to a time when a problem arose and no solution was in sight—not even a sliver of clarity. You prayed, reasoned, replayed scenarios, and still . . . nothing.

Isn't it wild how we believe that if we just think harder or worry more, the answer will appear? But anxiety doesn't fix what trust was meant to carry. Here's the truth: We were never designed to bear the weight of divine responsibility. That's God's territory, not ours. Our grip can feel tight, our striving sincere, but control was never the invitation. Surrender was.

The heart was wired to rest in God's ability, not crack under the pressure of its own. When we let Him take the lead, we're freed to be faithful without needing to figure it all out. What we see as uncertainty, He sees as setup. What we call delay, He's using for development. He's strengthening our roots, shaping our character, and preparing us for what's ahead.

Take a breath. Release the tension. God is already working behind the scenes in ways you can't yet imagine. You don't have to have the answers—just stay close to the One who is the solution.

day 99

What do you need to let go of today?

Dear Jesus, help me to remember that I am not in control, but You are. Let me rely on You with total confidence in Your good will for me. In Jesus's name, amen.

MORE THAN WORDS OR FEELINGS

Continue steadfastly in prayer,
being watchful in it with thanksgiving.
COLOSSIANS 4:2 ESV

Do you ever find yourself struggling to pray? You open your mouth, but it feels like you're speaking into empty space. Maybe the words don't come. Maybe they do—but they feel tired, repetitive, or hollow. Maybe you believe God can respond . . . but you're not convinced He will.

But prayer has never been about our feelings. It's about faith. Every time we turn our face toward heaven, we open the line of communication to the One who already knows, already cares, and always listens. Prayer isn't a vending machine or a cosmic suggestion box. It's powerful. It's personal. It's planted straight into the heart of God—and it never gets lost in translation.

Prayer reorients our distracted hearts. It slows our pace, silences the lies, and brings us back to what's true. It reminds us that God is holy—and that we are heard. That we are held. That we are not alone.

Even when the words feel weak or the answers feel delayed, prayer is still a declaration of trust. It tills the ground for miracles. It softens our pride. It fuels our hope. And often? It's the most powerful thing we can possibly do.

day 100

What does it look like for you to "continue steadfastly in prayer"? Write about how you might grow in consistency, attentiveness, and gratitude in your conversations with God.

Dear Jesus, open my heart to prayer. Give me faith to sit before You in stillness, even if my words are few and even if my feelings don't comply. In Jesus's name, amen.

ABOUT THE AUTHOR

CLEERE CHERRY REAVES is the owner and creator of Cleerely Stated, a successful product line that can be found online and in retail stores all over the United States. She is an author, speaker, and educator who is passionate about serving others and building God's kingdom. Well-known for her easy-to-relate-to, practical writing style, Cleere's mission is to help others see themselves and the world around them through the eyes of Jesus. Cleere now hosts a growing podcast called "Let's Be Cleere," where she hopes people are encouraged by the raw, real love of Jesus. She was born and raised in Greenville, North Carolina. She's a proud alumnus of the University of North Carolina at Chapel Hill and loves to live life to the fullest. Her favorite times always include her husband, Will, and their son, Sledge, who was born in July 2021.

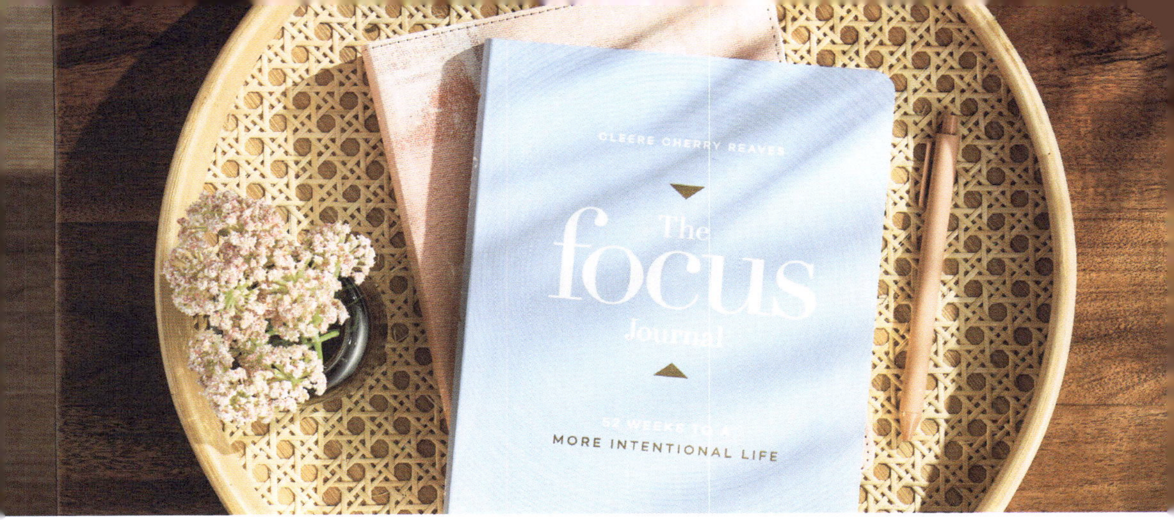

Looking for more from Cleere?

Check out her other DaySpring books
at your favorite retail store or on dayspring.com.

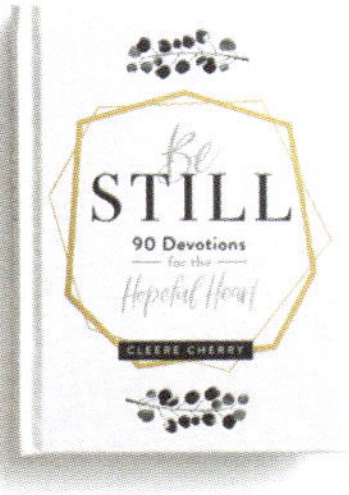

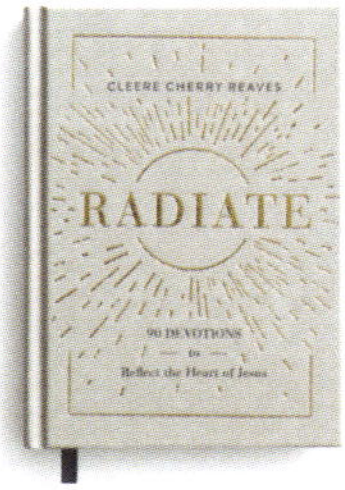

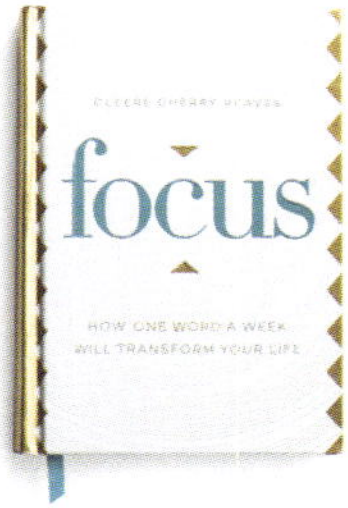

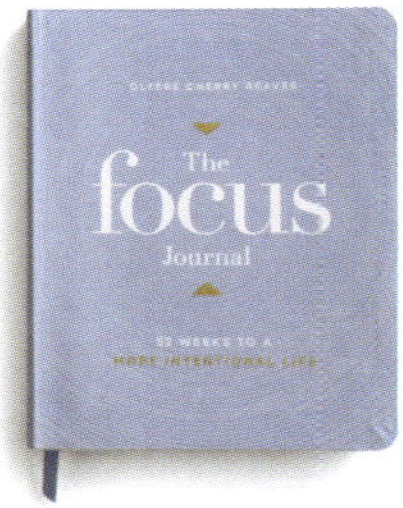

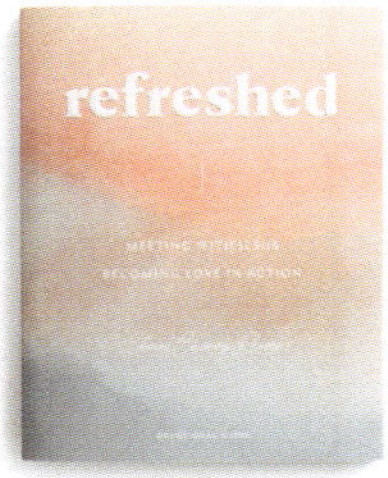

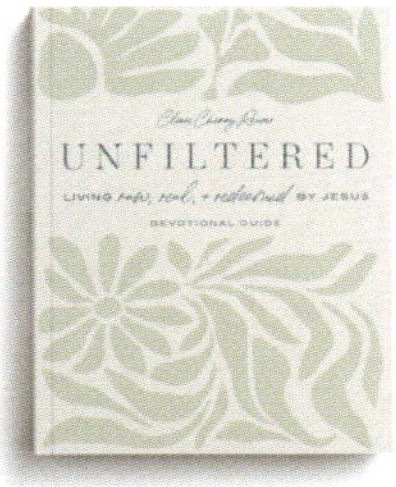

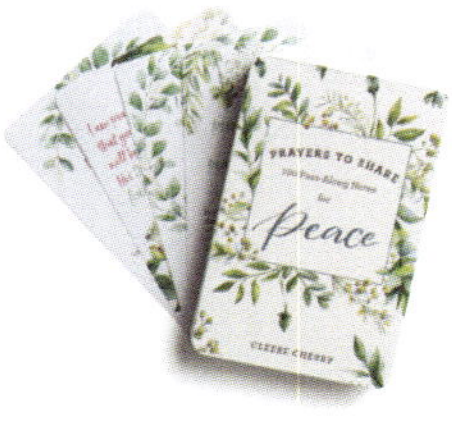

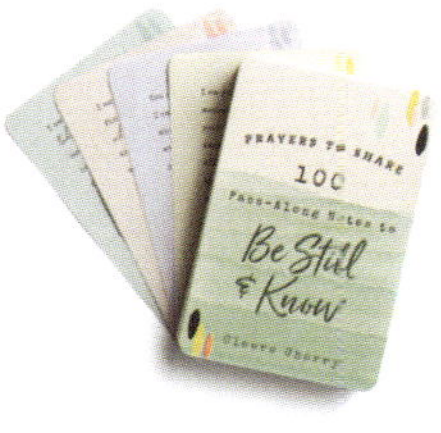

Dear Friend,

This book was prayerfully crafted with you, the reader, in mind. Every word, every sentence, every page was thoughtfully written, designed, and packaged to encourage you—right where you are this very moment. At DaySpring, our vision is to see every person experience the life-changing message of God's love. So, as we worked through rough drafts, design changes, edits, and details, we prayed for you to deeply experience His unfailing love, indescribable peace, and pure joy. It is our sincere hope that through these Truth-filled pages your heart will be blessed, knowing that God cares about you—your desires and disappointments, your challenges and dreams.

He knows. He cares. He loves you unconditionally.

BLESSINGS!
THE DAYSPRING BOOK TEAM